A SENSORY CURRICULUM
FOR VERY SPECIAL PEOPLE

HUMAN HORIZONS SERIES

A SENSORY CURRICULUM FOR VERY SPECIAL PEOPLE

A Practical Approach to Curriculum Planning

FLO LONGHORN

A CONDOR BOOK
SOUVENIR PRESS (E & A) LTD

This book is dedicated to
all the very special children and special people at Wren
Spinney School, Kettering, Northamptonshire, and
St John's School, Kempston, Bedford, Bedfordshire.
Without their inspiration and hard work, this book could
not have been published.

ACKNOWLEDGEMENTS

I would like to acknowledge the help and support of the following people who contributed their time, expertise, and love, to help in the writing of this book:

Anita Royall
Roger Hinds
Frances Palmer and the film crew from Video
   Communications
Roger Longhorn

and also:
Miles Pilling, Liz Clough, Christine Smith, Harry Clark, Andrea Lucas, Barry Kemp, Ann Stirzaker, Fabia Moore, and Charles Byrne.

Photography courtesy of Steve O'Donoghue, Bedford Mencap.

PREFACE

This book reflects work in the sensory curricula area currently
under way in special schools and other settings in the United
Kingdom. It is based on practical experience and reflects an on-
going, evolving, and changing sensory curriculum. Although it
is devised for the very special child or person, it will be of value
to a much wider audience, with suitable modifications or
alterations, to suit individual requirements.

The children and people referred to in this book are
individually described as 'the very special child' or 'the very
special person'. This description applies to those who have
profound, multiple learning difficulties, usually linked to
sensory and physical impairment. Such people are usually
unable to sense, manipulate and/or respond to their own
environment in order to learn from it.

CONTENTS

1   THE BEGINNING OF SENSORY LEARNING

Contents

1   What Are the Senses?

The senses comprise taste, smell, sound, vision, touch (tactile experience), and bodily experience. Something sensed via a combination of the senses is called a *multisensory experience*.

Look at these sensory clues and guess the object:

What Am I?
I feel smooth.
Fingers can enclose me.
I feel round.
I taste bitter.
I fit into a hand.
I am hard when bitten.
I am red.

I can roll along your arm.
You can hear me bounce near/far/behind and in front of
   you.
When you hit me I make a 'klunk' noise.
You can watch me go up and down/from side to side.
I smell of rubber.
You can feel a rush of air as I whizz past you.
If you reach in space you can touch me.
If you bend your arm and extend it, you can throw me.
I float on water.
I splash when thrown into water.

Answer: I am a red ball.

There are 21 sensory clues here to help a very special child
understand the concept of a ball. While only one or two clues
may give you the answer, the child needs a multisensory
approach to enable him to perceive the ball. Clues would be
given whenever a ball was used to help in understanding the
concept of a ball.
   Look at the following sensory clues and guess the activity:

What Am I Doing?
I can feel a liquid.
It feels warm.
I can feel bubbles.
They 'pop' on my hands.
They tickle my nose.
There is a smell of water/soap/soapy liquid.
I bend and stretch my arm to make the water move.
My fingers close and open to catch bubbles.

I can feel the edge of a bowl.
It feels round.
It is bigger than my hand.
The water in it comes up to my elbow.
It makes a swishy noise.
It makes a gurgly noise.
It tastes soapy.
I don't like the taste and pull a face.
I can make the water move.
I can see coloured patterns in the water.

In the water is an object.
It fills with water.
It pours out the water.
It is slippery.

Answer: I am washing the dishes.

The experience of very special children is a multisensory one. They need to use all the senses to understand what they are doing, whether it is playing with a ball or washing the dishes. They will generalise sensory experience from their sensory curriculum to help in perceiving the activity. This will take a long time and does not happen overnight.

For example, in a particular week a child may have experienced, with help:

Sense	*Experience*
tactile	warm/cold water touch experiences
smell	soapy smells
bodily experience	arm reaching for a noisy toy
bodily experience	fingers opening and closing on a glittery necklace
sound	listening to watery noises in the water tray
vision	watching bubbles being blown
taste	water tastes
bodily experience	helping blow bubbles

These sensory experiences help prepare the child to use his senses in every way to help in understanding the activity of washing dishes.

2   How do the Senses Evolve?

To understand the development of the use of senses, look at what a baby can achieve in the first few months of life. Like the very special child, there are many individual variations in the rate of sensory development in each baby. Not every baby reaches the same level of performance within the same time period.

Senses—before birth
In the womb, the baby has bodily movement provided by the

mother's movement, fluid, uterus, and placenta. It is stroked and massaged as the mother moves around. The baby floats in fluid that stimulates like a small whirlpool. It listens to the mother's heart-beat and body organs, plus sounds from 'outside'.

Taste

A 12-hour-old baby can enjoy sugar water placed on its tongue and pull a face at lemon juice.

Sound

A new-born baby's ears function before birth. Babies go to sleep faster to the record of a human heart-beat.

Smell

A new-born baby can smile at the smell of banana essence and pull faces at the smell of rotten eggs.

Vision

Given a choice, babies look at a chess-board surface rather than a plain one, bull's eye target rather than stripes, and in general prefer complex to simple patterns.

Sound

A baby can wriggle in rhythm to its mother's voice patterns.

Vision

Although a baby is born with 20/500 vision (nearly legally blind), at eight weeks old it can differentiate between shapes of objects as well as colours (generally red, followed by blue).

Sound

By the time they are born, most babies prefer female voices.

Vision

At three months, the baby begins to develop stereoscopic vision.

Bodily experience

At 12 days old, a baby can imitate an adult sticking out a tongue.

If it had a dummy in its mouth at the time, the baby can remember and stick its tongue out when the dummy is removed.

Sound

Within a few weeks of birth, babies recognise the sound of their mother's speech.

Vision

At two weeks old, babies can turn aside or squirm to avoid

being hit by an object moving quickly towards them.

If the object is on an angled path, which would miss them, the baby follows the motion with its eyes without signs of anxiety.

Bodily experience
A baby has the skill of being able to swim at birth, and, if held upright on a table, is nearly able to walk when suspended. Babies lose these skills and have to relearn them later.

At two months old, the baby smiles in fascination at a new discovery—its own hand. Eye/hand co-ordination develops between five and seven months. This is the point at which many developmental checklists begin.

It is clear that the very special child requires a sensory curriculum to help bring him to this important point. When the child reaches the stage of combining two sensory activities, such as vision and muscular action, then he can begin to perceive and use a more conventional curriculum. This is explored in Chapter 9: Extending the Sensory Curriculum.

3 What is a Sensory Curriculum?

A sensory curriculum is a part of a whole school curriculum or learning experience. It covers the development of the senses of taste, smell, touch (tactile experiences), vision, sound, and bodily experience. It also covers the development of the integration of all these senses to form a multisensory (or intermodal) approach for the child to use in learning situations. The importance of the senses was recorded as far back as 1866 by Edouard Seguin in his book *The Treatment of Idiocy by the Physiological Method.*

THE LINK TO OTHER AREAS OF THE CURRICULUM
The Sensory Curriculum provides the base for work in many other areas of the curriculum. Without the stimulation and awakening of the senses, it would be difficult for a very special child to begin to make sense of the outside world and begin to learn.

The very special child needs to receive as many sensory clues as possible in order to make sense of the curriculum being taught. Look at just one area of the curriculum—communication—to see how the senses can help a child to succeed:

Communication (giving and receiving of information)	*listening* to a range of sounds *feeling* vibratory instruments *looking* at a noisy toy *smelling* a wood and skin drum *looking* at lips moving *bouncing* to rhythms *feeling* a mouth move *blowing* bubbles

All these senses are helping a child to begin to understand the complex areas of communication.

4   Who Can Use a Sensory Curriculum?

The stimulation of the senses in order to help in the learning process is not limited to the very special child. It is applicable to a wide range of people at certain times during their lives. It may be used for all their lives, at specific periods of time, or intermittently. Each person is individual in his or her requirements. For example, it could cover:

Babies
   Babies require sensory stimulation from the moment of birth. Premature babies who have been in incubators need to catch up on the sensory stimulation they have missed.

Understimulated children
   Such children require an intensive period of sensory stimulation which they may have missed in their vital formative years.

A person with a failing sense
   The other senses require sharpening to help the person cope with a failing sense. An example of this is a boy with failing sight who loves art. He uses scented felt-tip pens to enhance his drawings which he cannot see. He also uses collage materials such as sand and beans to continue with his art.

A person who has been in a coma
   The senses may provide the missing link to memory and events in the past. The British Medical Association has a 'Coma Kit' for such use.

Older people
Older people may enjoy memories evoked by sensory experiences, especially if they are confined to an environment which does not promise a wide range of experiences, eg. a hospital or nursing home.

People in hospital settings
Sensory stimulation is important to people confined to a hospital setting with only 'hospital' sensory stimulation. They cannot use everyday experiences to gain a sensory awareness.

People leaving a hospital setting to rejoin the community
The sensory experiences of ordinary life are essential for people rejoining the community. A hospital setting does not provide these stimuli and awareness of the senses is required for living in the community.

Children with specific learning difficulties
The stimulation of the senses may help in the learning process for children with learning difficulties, eg. an intensive approach to the sense of sound, to encourage good listening skills.

People undergoing therapeutic treatment
The physiotherapist, occupational therapist, speech therapist, remedial gymnast, etc., can combine the treatment with sensory stimulation to make the treatment more meaningful. The treatment is made more interesting and has a dual learning process.

Always remember that each person is a unique individual whose sensory programme has to be individual, suitably tailored to his or her requirements and well monitored.

5 Planning a Sensory Curriculum
The Sensory Curriculum should be planned and developed in co-ordination with all other main areas of the curriculum. The Sensory Curriculum should *not* be viewed as an isolated part of the overall curriculum, *nor* as being more important than another area. It should form part of a well-balanced, overall curriculum, whose main aim is to meet the individual requirements of each child.

The Link to the Planning of the School Curriculum
Each school, under the direction of the Headteacher, will use

its own approach in planning the overall school curriculum. The Sensory Curriculum should be devised within the framework of the school curriculum. However, there may be a need for flexibility in approach, in view of the uniqueness of the Sensory Curriculum for the very special child.

PLANNING THE USE OF RESOURCES FOR A SENSORY CURRICULUM

Effective resources are required to back up a well planned sensory curriculum. The resources of time, space, material, and human resources are all equally important. These resources need on-going planning and develop as the curriculum evolves. They require regular monitoring and assessment. This monitoring means that any sensory resource not being fully used or wrongly used can be rethought and replanned.

THE MANAGEMENT OF SPACE

Each classroom has four walls and floor space over which staff have control and can effect change. The area can be carefully assessed and change made to enable the Sensory Curriculum to be taught effectively. No classroom space is ideal, but much can be done to make it realistic and functional for the requirements of the particular group in the room.

The classroom space does not end at the door. There are resources that can be utilised outside, providing this is negotiated with other staff, including the head. Examples of these additional resources are:

— a broom cupboard converted into a dark room (see Chapter 2).
— a long corridor wall turned into a long, exciting tactile wall, from the floor upwards.
— old sluice room converted into a rumpus room.
— a corner of a cloakroom for a very large cardboard box to use for light stimulation.
— a designated area in the school's music room for a sound stimulation area and tape library of a wide range of music.
— a jacuzzi put into the swimming pool area for vibration and body tactile awareness.
— a piece of ground outside the room planted for seasonal colour, textures, and smells, including pot herbs.

The space in a classroom can be simply designed by following the Space Action Checklist below. Examples of room plans can be seen in Figures 1a and 1b.

Space Management—Action Checklist

1   Draw a rough floor plan of your room as if it was empty.
2   Indicate, by dotted lines, the movement routes in the room.
3   Write down six to eight important curriculum areas for your particular group.
4   Now look at your floor plan. Name and colour areas to use for the identified curriculum areas. Lack of space may lead to a dual use for space, eg. tactile in the nurture area.
5   Consult with others, showing them your room plan for constructive help.
6   Identify hidden potential in your room, in the school, in the community.
7   Evaluate the space regularly, and modify as required.
8   Develop hidden potential areas carefully and with consultation.
9   Look at the furniture. Is it functional? Is it used or just cluttering the room? Do you really need a large desk right in the middle of the room?
10   Link a space with clues to let the special child know you are there, eg. a consistent sound, smell, colour, or texture will give the child an idea of what is expected of him.
11   Pay attention to beauty in the room to uplift the child, staff, and visitors.
12   Try different levels in the room, such as a safe platform so that children gain a variety of interesting views of their environment, not just at feet level.
13   Some equipment can be used at different times of the year. For example, a mobile bolster swing when it is too cold to go outside, a play pen full of autumn leaves to roll in, or a cool fan during the summer months.
14   Ask your friendly local architect into school to help in planning your space. They are the experts.
15   Encourage others to use the spaces in the room as it lessens isolation and encourages interaction.

Fig. 1a. Room space plan

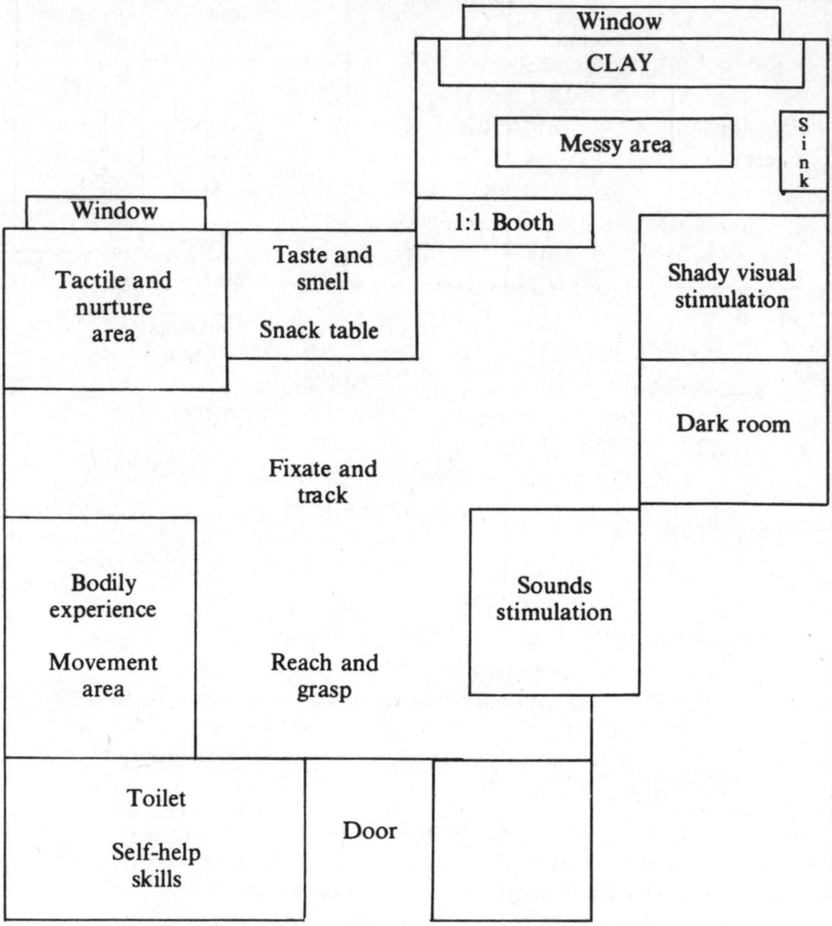

NOTES: Taste and smell are near the snack table.
Bodily experience incorporates reach/grasp/fixate and track.
Nurture and tactile are combined.
The dark room is one half of the stock cupboard.
The 1:1 booth is for a stimuli-free area.

Fig. 1b. Room space plan

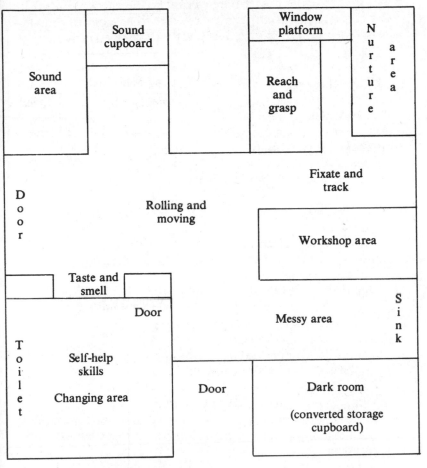

NOTES: Messy area is near the sink.

Self-help skills are taught in context in the changing/toilet area.

Nurture area is curtained off and has a window platform.

A store cupboard outside the room is now the dark room.

USE OF TIME IN PLANNING THE SENSORY CURRICULUM

Once the space and resources have been planned, it is important to look at how the use of time can make the curriculum work most effectively. Lack of time is often used as a cover for inefficiency, delays and failures. Time has to be planned in five areas:

Supporting staff time

Analyse how supporting staff use time.

Are these staff used efficiently? (Try a time log and analysis —see Appendix C).

Have they a clear timetable?

Is there a timetable for volunteers?

Are volunteers used effectively?

Are timetables adhered to most of the time?

Your time

How do you organise your day, week, half-term?

What do you do all day?

Can you delegate and make your time more effective?

Have you tried a daily time log and analysis (see Appendix C)?

The child's time

What does the child do all day long?

Try a daily time log and analysis (see Appendix C).

Try a curriculum planner (see Appendix C).

Check a week of time use.

Plan a child's individual timetable and keep to it, integrate it into the class and school timetable.

Thinking Time

Thinking and planning are crucial to the development of any curriculum and resources. We think at about 600 words per minute as opposed to 200 words per minute for reading. Lateral or creative thinking brings the extra quality to any planning if time is allowed to do this. Thinking time should be valued and planned for accordingly.

Time and room management

Room management systems can also enhance the use of time. Staff have very clear roles to enable time to be used effectively, both in a one-to-one relationship and in groups. Room management needs to be clearly thought out as it is very demanding to maintain. (Coles and Blunden, McBrien and Weightman, Porterfield).

PLANNING MATERIAL AND HUMAN RESOURCES FOR USE WITH THE
SENSORY CURRICULUM

Material Resource 'Banks'
Having considered the resources of space and time, one must
now look at material resources. For example, it is hard to
follow a regular individual taste programme if the materials are
not at hand, the tastes have gone mouldy, the individual
taste session is not on anyone's timetable, etc.

Resource banks should match and enhance the Sensory
Curriculum. They must be kept up to date and should be
maintained easily to hand. It is useful to allocate responsibility
to members of staff for various areas to check the resources
regularly, replenishing and/or repairing equipment, and
locating new resources.

An ideal storage unit for the 'bank' is a mobile trolley with
trays clearly marked and kept tidy. Large toy boxes are good
for outside equipment. Another form of sensory bank is a set of
shelves in a corridor. Someone should have overall responsibility
for the resource shelves, as they have more general use.

Some children require their own individual resource banks.
The contents of two typical resource banks are listed below:

Susan requires objects she can hold or wear and bring to her
face to observe. Her resource bank is a box containing:
   smelly soaps
   sand-filled frog
   diffractive lid of a box
   tinsel
   piece of crackly red paper
   glitter glove
   gold bracelets
   duck puppet

Katie requires objects she can hold and observe, but which will
discourage mouthing. Her resource box contains:
   Brillo pad
   two-sided scrubbing brush
   prickly hedgehog
   piece of very stiff net
   nylon stocking full of sand
   carbolic soap

yellow scouring pad
(all items are observed during use for suitability)

Human Resources

Without adequate human back-up, the Sensory Curriculum is not going to work. Because of the nature of their handicaps, very special children are inevitably going to require intensive human input. The effective use of these human resources is imperative. They all add up to give a new human dimension to the Sensory Curriculum. The following are some human resources and ways they can be used:

Headteacher

Headteachers should have a finger on the pulse of the school and on the purse strings. They should be involved in helping to plan the resources, should be approached with enthusiasm, and should be kept up to date on sensory developments. They should be excellent teachers and should be invited to teach with you. They will then appreciate that it is just as important to buy a vibrating foot spa as it is to buy a new netball post.

Supporting staff

They may have outside hobbies or pursuits that can be used as resources. Examples are the staff member who has a herb garden and makes *pot-pourri*, or the teacher who enjoys sewing and will make glittery gloves. They may have friends who will add a resource, such as a scrounger of free materials, a bass player, or a yoga enthusiast.

Family resources

It goes without saying that the more the family is effectively involved in school and the curriculum, the more the very special child will gain from the curriculum. The home resources can provide the necessary one-to-one relationship for movement sessions, or they could organise a sensory section in the school toy library. They can take the sensory curriculum philosophy home and generalise it from a school setting.

Volunteers

Volunteers need special roles within the Sensory Curriculum and need careful monitoring. While they may not have the expertise to assess and plan, they can offer a new approach to working with the senses and another chance for sensory experience to be generalised. Volunteers prefer to come in for a specific directed session rather than hang around with the feeling that they are getting in the way.

Students

Many schools now train students to work in the area of severe to profound learning disabilities. They require clear guidelines and timetables. They can also be encouraged to write their reports or study papers on specific sensory areas, giving a new insight into their use.

Advisers or inspectors

There are a range of such people in each county to advise and help in specific areas of the curriculum. They are accountable to help with the development of the curriculum in your room. They require careful handling and encouragement, but can be very helpful as they have an overview of the curriculum at a county and national level. Invite them in to observe and plan. For example, a drama adviser came to run lunchtime sessions, linked to a drama teacher in a middle school, started a pairing of students in drama and provided funding for a drama company to do a two-day workshop. This all followed one day of observation in a class for very special children.

6   Learning How to Teach a Sensory Curriculum

The very special child requires considerable help and support in the learning situation, whether formal or informal. Careful thought has to be given to how the child learns best and the optimum situation in which he can learn to use his senses. The following examples demonstrate the problems in various areas.

Smell   It is of little use to place a child near a vase of flowers and expect him to smell them.
             You must position the child comfortably, bring the flowers up to his nose, tell him what he is smelling, and let him touch the flowers.
Taste   Do not put a taste onto the tongue and expect him to taste it.
             You must position the child comfortably, encourage him to smell the taste first, tell him

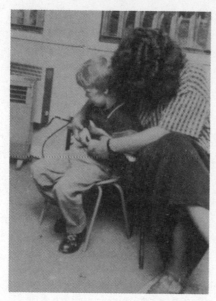 

(*Left*) The adult helps Tom to learn in a 'co-active' situation, lending her body to help him with his task. (*Right*) Now she is using 'co-operative' learning, gently encouraging his hand to use the beater on the chime bars. Tom is concentrating hard on the activity and doing most of the work himself.

	what he is tasting, and encourage tongue and mouth movements.
Sound	You cannot leave bells next to a child and expect him to make a sound and listen.
	You must position the child comfortably, tie bells to his arms or legs, and encourage movement and listening to the noise being made.
Bodily Movement	You cannot put a child on a trampoline and expect him to move.
	You must get on the trampoline with the child, experience the bouncing together, explain what is happening.
Touch	You cannot lie a child under an autumn tree and expect him to touch and feel the falling leaves.
	You must roll him, push him, throw leaves over

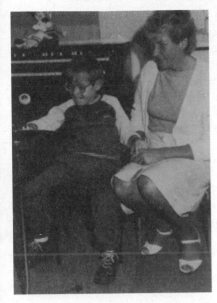

Paul learns in a 'reactive' situation. The adult encourages him through praise and Paul works independently.

Simon shows his own 'preference' learning by choosing to make his own sounds on the guitar, when given a choice of instruments.

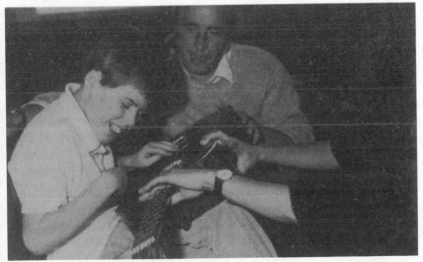

Vision

him, build a pile of leaves together and feel the texture of the leaves, the tree bark, the soil, etc. You cannot switch on a torch in the dark room and expect him to look at the light.

You must position the child comfortably, reassure him, tell him what is going to happen, show pleasurable anticipation for the expected torch flash, move the beam up and down, side-to-side, etc.

This special way of learning can be broken down into four stages of simple learning. It is not isolated, meaningless or mechanical learning. It is *interactive*, to help motivate the very special child to learn and explore his or her sensory environment (Glenn and Cunningham).

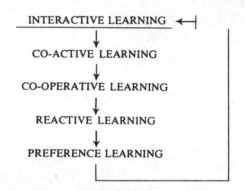

INTERACTIVE LEARNING
↓
CO-ACTIVE LEARNING
↓
CO-OPERATIVE LEARNING
↓
REACTIVE LEARNING
↓
PREFERENCE LEARNING

INTERACTIVE LEARNING

Stage 1: Co-active Learning
The adult or caring person lends her body and mind to the child for the learning situation. It is a one-to-one situation where there is usually total dependence on the adult. The adult moves the child into positions to help him learn or moves body parts so that he experiences learning by 'doing'.

Stage 2: Co-operative Learning
When the child is ready for less dependence, then he can begin to learn co-operatively. The adult or caring person begins to perform alongside the child in a very encouraging and supportive role. This happens in tiny stages. The adult

holds an elbow instead of a hand, moves her body away from sitting with the child, etc.

Stage 3: Reactive Learning

As the child gains more confidence, the stage he now moves into is reactive learning. This means that gradually he accepts that he has the skills to learn by himself. He can be encouraged in the normal way—by a smile, verbal praise, or a hug. He may not reach this stage in every area, but he can begin to learn by himself for short periods of time, in the areas where he feels most confident.

Stage 4: Preference Learning

When the very special child can learn independently in some areas, he can enter learning experiences selected by himself. This means that he is given a choice of learning activities and can actively choose what *he* wants to learn. He is given control of his own learning situation and shows preference for one or more learning tasks.

It is important to remember that some children will need much help in being able to make a choice. This is because their physical handicaps preclude them being fully independent. They may always need the physical help and guidance, described as 'co-active learning'. However, they may well be able to show preference learning and the observation skills of the staff in recognising the child's potential are essential.

For example, some children could use preference learning through a switch controlling a computer. They require discreet assistance and acknowledgement, through careful observation, of the stages they may have reached.

The remaining chapters of this book offer help in planning individual Sensory Curriculum areas for visual, taste, smell, sound, touch, and bodily experience, as well as for multisensory experiences. The final two chapters cover ways of extending the Sensory Curriculum into other more sophisticated areas. The examples used are guidelines only, and should not be seen as meeting every requirement for a Sensory Curriculum.

Each school will devise a unique, tailor-made, Sensory Curriculum to meet its own requirements. I hope that the examples presented, taken from practical, real-life experiences, will help.

School Action Plan

LOOK AT YOURSELF
Now
think hard
LOOK AT YOUR GROUP
LOOK AT YOUR STAFF
LOOK AT EACH CHILD
LOOK AT YOUR CURRICULUM
LOOK AT YOUR RESOURCES
LOOK AT YOUR PARENTS
LOOK AT YOUR VOLUNTEERS/HELPERS
LOOK AT YOUR SPACE
LOOK AT YOUR TIME
Look at your
outside agencies
LOOK AT YOUR HEADTEACHER

7   Helpful Books and Articles for Planning a Sensory Curriculum

The following references may help in planning your Sensory Curriculum.

THE SENSES AND PERCEPTION

Bower, T. (1977). *The Perceptual World of the Child.* London: Fontana Books.

Legge and Barber (1976). *Perception and Information.* London: Methuen.

Webb, R. C. (1969). 'Sensory-Motor Training of the Profoundly Retarded', in *American Journal of Mental Deficiency*, vol. 74, pp. 283–95.

DEVELOPMENT OF A NORMAL BABY

Brazelton, T. B. (1972). *Infants and Mothers.* London: Hutchinson.

Carter, M. (ed.) (1982). *Baby's First Year of Life.* Oxford: The Oxford Illustrated Press.

Friedrich, O. (1983). 'Secrets of a Baby's Mind', in *Time Magazine,* 15th August, 1983, pp. 40–7.
Leech, P. (1974). *Babyhood.* Harmondsworth: Penguin Books.
Verry, T. (1982). *The Secret Life of the Unborn Child.* Hamilton.

MANAGEMENT SKILLS
Bailey, I. J. (1983). *Structuring a Curriculum for Profoundly Mentally Handicapped Children.* Chapter 6 on Management. Obtainable from: Publications Department, Jordanhill College of Education, Southbrae Drive, Glasgow, Scotland.
There is also a good, reasonably priced set of booklets on aspects of management, available from: The Industrial Society, P.O. Box 1BQ, Robert Hyde House, 48 Bryanston Square, London W1A 1BQ. Titles include:
   The Manager's Responsibility for Communication
   The Manager as a Leader
   Delegation
   Chairmanship and Discussion Leading
   Effective Use of Time
Kiernan, C., Reid, B., and Goldbart, J. (1987). *Foundations of Communication and Language* (staff training package). Manchester University Press.
Sebba, J. (1988). *The Education of People with Profound and Multiple Handicaps: Resource materials for staff training.* Manchester University Press.

COMPLEX LEARNING DIFFICULTIES
Best, A. B. (1987). *Steps to Independence: Practical Guidelines on Teaching People with Mental and Sensory Handicaps.* Kidderminster: British Institute of Mental Handicap.
Brudenell, P. (1986). *The Other Side of Profound Handicap.* London: Macmillan.
Coupe, J., and Porter, J. (1986). *The Education of Children with Severe Learning Difficulties: Bridging the Gap between Theory and Practice.* London: Croom Helm.
Ellis, D. (1986). *Sensory Impairments in Mentally Handicapped People.* London: Croom Helm.
Evans, P., and Ware, J. (1986). *Education Provision for Children in Special Care Units.* Windsor: NFER-Nelson.

Evans, P., and Ware, J. (1987). *Special Care Provision: The Education of Children with Profound and Multiple Learning Difficulties.* Windsor: NFER-Nelson.

Glenn, S., and Cunningham, C. 'Special Care but Active Learning', in *Special Education: Forward Trends,* vol. 11, no. 4.

Hogg, J., Lambe, L., Cowie, J., and Coxon, J. (1987). *People with profound retardation and multiple handicaps attending schools and social education centres.* London: Mencap.

Hogg, J., and Sebba, J. (1986). *Profound Retardation and Multiple Impairment,* Volume 11, 'Education and Therapy'. London: Croom Helm.

Seguin, E. (1866). *Idiocy and its Treatment by the Physiological Method.* New York: William Woods & Co.

Valetutti P. J. (1984). *Severely and Profoundly Handicapped Students: Their Nature and Their Needs.* Manchester: Haigh & Hochland.

Teaching the Multiply Handicapped (1980). Prepared by the Walsall Working Party on Curriculum Development for the Mentally Handicapped (ESN(S)) Child. Walsall Education Authority.

Webb, R. C. (1969). 'Sensory-Motor Training of the Profoundly Retarded', in *American Journal of Mental Deficiency,* No. 74, pp. 283-95.

Wehman, P. (1979). *Curriculum Design for the Severely and Profoundly Handicapped.* New York: Human Science Press.

Wyman, R. (1986). *Multiply Handicapped Children.* London: Souvenir Press.

PLANNING THE STYLE AND CONTENT (*of a Sensory Curriculum*)

Ainscow, M., and Tweddle, D. (1979). *Preventing Learning Failure: An Objectives Approach.* New York: John Wiley and Sons, Inc.

Bailey, I. J. (1983). *Structuring a Curriculum for Profoundly Mentally Handicapped Children.* Obtainable from Publications Department, Jordanhill College of Education, Southbrae Drive, Glasgow, Scotland.

Burton, T. A. (1981). 'Deciding what to teach the severely/profoundly retarded student: a teacher responsibility', in *Educating and Training of the Mentally Retarded*, vol. 16, part 1, pp. 74-9.

Eden, D. J. (1976). *Mental Handicap*. London: George Allen & Unwin.
Kiernan, C. (1981). *Analysis of Programmes for Teaching*. Globe Educational.
Mittler, P. (1979). *People Not Patients*. London: Methuen.
Morgenstern, F. (1981). *Teaching Plans for Handicapped Children*. London: Methuen.
Norris, D. (1982). *Profound Mental Handicap*. Costello Educational.
Perkins, E. A. *et al. Helping the Retarded*. Kidderminster: British Institute of Mental Handicap.
Presland, J. L. (1980). 'Educating Special Care Children: A Review of the literature', in *Educational Research*, no. 23, pp. 20-23.
Rectory Paddock School (1983). *In Search of a Curriculum* (2nd ed.). Obtainable from: Robin Wren Publications, 2, Merrilees Road, Sidcup, Kent.
Simon, G. B. (1981). *The Next Step on the Ladder*. Kidderminster: British Institute of Mental Handicap.
Wehman, P. (1979): *Curriculum Design for the Severely and Profoundly Handicapped*. New York: Human Sciences Press.

MANAGEMENT OF SPACE/TIME RESOURCES

Atherton, B. (1980). *Adapting Spaces for Resource Based Learning*. Obtainable from: Council for Educational Technology, 3, Devonshire Street, London W1N 2BA.
Bartholomew, L. (1980). 'Special Care Units: The Shape of Things to Come?' in *Apex*, vol. 8, no. 2, pp. 48-50.
Bayes, K., and Franklin, S. (1971); *Designing for the Handicapped*. George Godwin.
Coles, E., and Blunden, R. (1979). 'Establishment and Maintenance of a Ward Based Activity Period within a Mental Handicap Hospital', in *Research Report No. 8*, Mental Handicap in Wales, Cardiff.
Glover, E., and Mesibov, G. B. (1978). 'An Interest Center Sensory Stimulation Program for Severely and Profoundly Retarded Children', in *Education and Training of the Mentally Retarded*, vol. 13, part 2, pp. 172-6.
Harding, T. *The Role of a Constructional Furniture System in Special Schools*. Obtainable from: H.P.R.U., Newcastle-upon-Tyne Polytechnic.

McBrien, J., and Weightman, J. (1980). 'The Effect of Room Management Procedure on the Engagement of Profoundly Retarded Children', in *British Journal of Mental Subnormality*, vol. 50, pp. 38-46.

Porterfield, J., Blunden, R., and Blewitt, E. (1980). 'Improving Environments for Profoundly Handicapped Adults', in *Behaviour Modification*, vol. 4, pp. 225-41.

Sandhu, J. S. (1976). *Environmental Design for Handicapped Children*. London: Saxon House.

Sandhu, J. S., and Hendricks, J. H. (1974). *Special Schools Environments for Handicapped Children*. Obtainable from the Built Environment Group, School of Environment, Central London Polytechnic.

Ware, J. and Evans, P. (1986). Interactions between Profoundly Handicapped Pupils and Staff in a Special Care Class', in *Science and Service in Mental Retardation*, edited by Berg, J. M., and De Long, J. London: Methuen.

Westling, D. L., Ferrell, K., and Swenson, K. (1982). 'Intra Classroom Comparison of Two Arrangements for Teaching Profoundly Mentally Retarded Children', in *American Journal of Mental Deficiency*, 1982, vol. 86, no. 6, pp. 601-8.

CATALOGUES OF USEFUL EQUIPMENT AND BOOKS

Barnums Novelties,
67 Hammersmith Road,
London W14 8UY.

Shimmering curtains, masks, balloons, glitter powder, crowns, tiaras, etc.

Disabled Living Foundation,
380/384 Harrow Road,
London W9 2HU.

Information and equipment in many areas. Visits can be arranged.

EduPlay Toys,
Units H and I,
Vulcan Business Centre,
Vulcan Road,
Leicester LE5 3EBO.

Well made, good sized toys and equipment, including mirror chime mobile, and music activity centre.

Handicapped Persons Research Unit Newcastle-upon-Tyne Polytechnic, 1 Coach Lane, Newcastle-upon-Tyne NE7 7TW.	Range of books.
Mencap Bookshop, 123 Golden Lane, London EC1Y 0RT.	
Souvenir Press Ltd, 43 Great Russell Street, London WC1B 3PA.	Excellent range of relevant books.
T F H, 76 Barracks Road, Sandy Lane Industrial Estate, Stourport on Severn, Worcs. DY13 9QB.	Their range includes computer aids, sound carpet and bubble, vibro bubble, aroma disk player, etc.
Tridias, The Ice House, 124 Walcot Street, Bath BA1 5BG.	A vast range of glittery, gaudy novelties, such as water pistols, fake noses, duck quackers, sparkle wheel, etc.
The Consortium, Jack Tizard School, Finlay Street, London SW6 6HB.	A range of materials including Tac Pac, Galaxies, Seaside and Funfair materials.
Winslow Press, Telford Road, Bicester, Oxon OX6 0TS.	A wide selection of materials including language, social skills and age appropriate equipment.

2 DEVELOPING A VISUAL STIMULATION AND PREFERENCE CURRICULUM AND A VISUAL PREFERENCE BANK

Contents

1 Introduction

Vision is the major co-ordinating sense, as most sensory impressions have a visual input. For example, visual stimulation is an important part of the overall impression of:

— a furry animal which you are stroking,
— the jam doughnut you are eating,
— the cymbals making a crashing sound,
— the sweet-smelling lilac,
— the hammock you are swinging in.

The very special child may have the use of vision, but may not know how to use that sense, nor how to interpret the scenes that he is seeing. The child may be unable to use his vision to begin to explore the immediate surroundings. The child may have no incentive to experiment with his environment because no visual preference is being exhibited. A Visual Preference Programme can be used in two ways:

It can stimulate any vision that the child has by using intensive stimuli in order to gain a child's visual attention and co-operation. This may be fleeting, and one way of gaining attention is by use of a Dark Room.

It can link the visual stimulation of a child to the natural situations in his day-to-day life. For example, at feeding time there is both visual attention and human contact; 'peek-a-boo' play focuses attention on the human face, and, when singing, he can watch lips move and make sounds.

Every opportunity should be used to generalise the intensive Visual Stimulation Programme into the child's daily life. He may then begin to show spontaneous visual preference, which the programme should then reinforce in any way possible.

2 Planning a Visual Stimulation and Preference Curriculum

SETTING YOUR AIMS

The main aim for a Visual Stimulation and Preference Curriculum is to stimulate the child's vision to the fullest extent, in order to encourage the child to begin to look spontaneously and to regard his external environment.

SETTING YOUR GOALS

The goals to be set in the Visual Stimulation Curriculum should not be seen as graduated steps. There cannot be a developmental set of goals in visual stimulation, which varies so much from person to person.

Each individual has very personal inclinations regarding the materials, scenes, etc., which stimulate his or her vision. The enormous range of paintings in an art gallery verifies this fact. Very special children are no different, with personal preferences for a certain range of visual stimuli. The visual stimulation goals to be set should not be set in isolation, but should be integrated with other areas of the curriculum.

The use of vision is a major co-ordinating sense in most areas of the curriculum. For example, the sensory goal of 'reaching for a glittering mobile' is closely linked to other curriculum areas, such as attention, motivation, hand-eye co-ordination, and cause and effect.

The main goals may include some of the following:
— fun and enjoyment,
— stimulation,
— acceptance of a range of visual stimulation,
— beginning a controlled range of eye, head and body movements,
— beginning 'hand-to-eye' movements,
— beginning 'hand-out-to-touch' movements,
— beginning 'hand-out-to-grasp' movements,
— increased toleration to physical handling,
— beginning to vocalise,
— developing a visual memory,
— beginning to understand cause and effect,
— attention,
— beginning to use vision as a co-ordinating sense,
— simple discrimination,
— beginning to distinguish figure/ground.

Only one or two of these goals would be selected for a very special child. When the goal has been achieved, then another can be added to the curriculum.

PLANNING VISUAL STIMULATION CURRICULUM UNITS

The first steps of a simple Visual Stimulation Programme

could include the following areas:
  light preference
  flickering
  hands
  human face
  mouthing
  approaches to a child
  hand-watching
Example curriculum units follow below:

CURRICULUM DATA
Range of Light

Curriculum area	:	Cognitive
Main objective	:	Sensory development
Stage	:	Visual preference—range of light
Resources	:	RNIB adviser, dark room, orthoptist, school curriculum

---

1 Indifferent to any lights.
2 Shows a preference towards bright light from a window.
3 Shows a preference towards a range of very bright, intense lights.
4 Shows a preference towards prism effect.
5 Shows a preference towards glittering, reflective, and refractive objects.
6 Shows a preference towards fluorescent materials.
7 Shows a preference towards TV monitor close to face, with intense light programmes.
8 Other.

CURRICULUM DATA
Flickering

Curriculum area	:	Cognitive
Main objective	:	Sensory development
Stage	:	Visual preference—flickering
Resources	:	RNIB adviser, dark room, orthoptist, school curriculum

1   Indifferent to a range of flickering.
2   Reacts to bright light on/off.
3   Reacts to light in first instance, but not afterwards.
4   Shows preference for a range of flickers.
5   Creates own flickers through hands and fingers, or by moving the body.
6   Other.

CURRICULUM DATA
Hands

Curriculum area : Cognitive
Main objective   : Sensory development
Stage   : Visual preference—hands
Resources   : RNIB adviser, dark room, orthoptist, school curriculum

---

1   Indifferent to any hands.
2   Reacts to moving, 'flickering' hands near the face.
3   Reacts to hands covered in glittering gloves, silver markings, fluorescent paint.
4   Reacts to moving hands towards and away from the face.
5   Reacts to own hands close to face, illuminated with torch.
6   Moves own decorated, illuminated hands in front of face.
7   Other.

CURRICULUM DATA
Human Face

Curriculum area : Cognitive
Main objective   : Sensory development
Stage   : Visual preference—human face
Resources   : RNIB adviser, dark room, orthoptist, school curriculum

---

1   Indifferent to any face.
2   Reacts to very familiar face close up.
3   Reacts to faces close up.
4   Reacts to faces at a distance.

5 Follows a familiar face as it moves.
6 Moves towards familiar face.
7 Other.

CURRICULUM DATA
Mouthing

Curriculum area : Cognitive
Main objective   : Sensory development
Stage   : Visual preference—mouthing
Resources   : RNIB adviser, dark room, orthoptist, school curriculum

1 Objects to mouth.
2 Mouth to objects.
3 Exploration of objects with:
    a) tongue—licking,
    b) sucking—biting,
    c) chewing,
    d) using lips,
    e) spittle,
    f) other.

CURRICULUM DATA
Approaches to Child

Curriculum area : Cognitive
Main objective   : Sensory development
Stage   : Visual preference—approaches to child
Resources   : RNIB adviser, dark room, orthoptist, school curriculum

1 Indifferent to approaches.
2 Startles on approach.
3 Begins to frown on an approach.
4 Flinches on an approach.
5 Reacts favourably to an approach, smiles, turns head, turns body.
6 Discriminates on different approaches.
7 Begins own approach to people:

a) begins to use non-verbal communication,
b) stretches a hand or arm,
c) moves eyes,
d) wiggles,
e) smiles,
f) coos.
8 Other.

CURRICULUM DATA
Hand-watching

Curriculum area : Cognitive
Main objective : Sensory development
Stage : Visual preference—hand-watching
Resources : RNIB adviser, dark room, orthoptist, school curriculum

---

1 No apparent awareness of body.
2 No apparent awareness of hands or arms.
3 Movement of hands and arms in random patterns.
4 Movement of hands towards face.
5 Knocking of face with hands.
6 Movement of head towards hands.
7 Purposeful movement of hands near/on face.
8 Wriggling of hands/fingers near eyes.
9 Begins poking eyes.
10 Fleeting fixation of moving hands.
11 Tracking of hands near face.
12 Tracking of hands away from face.
13 Other.

Success in the areas so far mentioned may eventually lead to curriculum requirements in the following, more accepted, areas of visual stimulation:

attention   tracking   grasping
fixation   reaching   reaching and
visual   eye-hand   grasping
   discrimination   co-ordination

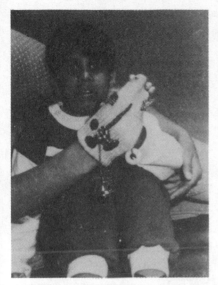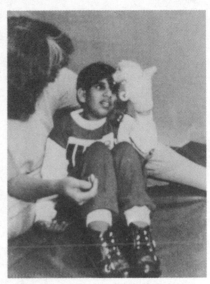

Despite lots of encouragement (*left*), Waqaus does not look at the glitter glove on the adult's hand, but when it is put on his own hand (*right*), he is more interested and watches as his hand makes the glove move.

However, the very special child may not reach these levels. Here are examples of two of these more advanced areas—fixation and tracking.

CURRICULUM DATA
Fixation

Curriculum area	:	Cognitive
Main objective	:	Sensory development
Stage	:	Visual preference—fixation
Resources	:	RNIB adviser, dark room, orthoptist, school curriculum

---

1 Change in facial expression.
   When a bright object is put in front of the child, the response is a change in facial expression or the child goes quiet or grows more excited, but no fixation.

2 Fixation—with corrections.
The child fixates and eyes drift away. Child keeps correcting the eyes.

3 Fixation—bright objects (or illuminated).
The child fixates for three seconds or more.

4 Fixation—low contrast.
The child fixates on a non-illuminated object for at least three seconds.

5 Other.

CURRICULUM DATA
Tracking

Curriculum area : Cognitive
Main objective : Sensory development
Stage : Visual preference—tracking
Resources : RNIB adviser, dark room, orthoptist, school curriculum

1 Horizontal tracking.
The object is held near the child's eye level until the child fixates. Then move object from side to side.

2 Vertical tracking.
As above, only up and down movement of the object.

3 Circular tracking.   •
Move the object in a slow circle of about one metre.

4 Irregular tracking.
Move objects in slow curves and angular movements for about ten seconds.

5 Tracking different length from eyes. (Including other side of room.)

6 Other.

---

3 Linking the Child to the Visual Stimulation and Preference Programme

THE FAMILY CAN HELP

The majority of a child's visual stimulation experiences happen at home or in other caring environments. Information from the home is an excellent basis on which to begin building a Visual

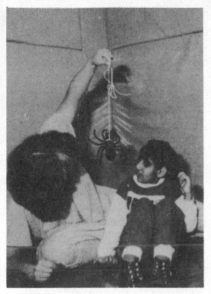

Waqaus looks at the spider (*left*), fixating his gaze on it. Now he tracks the spider (*right*) and spontaneously reaches upwards to grab at it.

Stimulation Programme and setting realistic goals for the child.

A simple sensory questionnaire should be completed by the family so that they are involved in the Visual Stimulation Programme at home, as well as at school. (See Appendix A for a sample Sensory Questionnaire).

A parent workshop in the area of visual stimulation will help to explain the aims of this particular sensory area, and will further involve the family.

'Visual stimulation' homework can be sent home occasionally for the child. Families usually rise to the challenge—especially siblings. Homework could be a request for the child to have a very shiny mobile suspended near his face, to see and to touch. Another homework assignment might include a flickering disco lamp sent home from school for the family to use with the child. (See Appendix B for a sample Homework Record.)

THE SCHOOL CAN HELP

Information at school can be collected using a simple recording form (see Appendix C for Simple Record Keeping). This form should be kept for a given period of time, during which a range of visual stimulations are presented to the child. The record will provide on-going information on the child's development in this sensory area.

There are a variety of assessment tools that can help in observing a child's use of vision. These are listed at the end of the chapter.

There are numerous reactions and non-reactions to be observed and used as the first step in an individual Visual Stimulation Programme. Some children's reactions will be the complete opposite of what might be expected. The overall knowledge and understanding of a child will help in interpreting what the child is telling you.

The following example curriculum sheet shows some of the ranges of reactions you may observe in a Visual Stimulation recording, based on a child's reactions to a variety of lights.

CURRICULUM DATA
Range of Reactions

Curriculum area	:	Cognitive
Main objective	:	Sensory development
Stage	:	Visual preference—reactions to light
Resources	:	RNIB adviser, stage one curriculum, orthoptist

RANGE OF REACTIONS

1   No preference.
2   Startles.
3   Stills.
4   Facial changes.
   a)   Closes eyes.
   b)   Rapid eye movement.
   c)   Mouth and tongue movements.
   d)   Follows movement with eyes.
5   Movement changes.
   a)   Hands in front of eyes.

  b) Rubs eyes/pokes eyes.
  c) Moves head.
  d) Arm movement, reaches for light.
  e) Moves legs.
  f) Kicks.
  g) Bounces.
6 Noise expressions.
  a) Cries or moans.
  b) Coos or laughs.
  c) Babbles.
7 Other.

THE CHILD CAN HELP

The child helps indirectly through your observations of him in each session. These observations will provide the foundation for an individual Visual Stimulation Programme. An example of how a child provides this information can be seen at the end of this chapter, in the section by Anita Royall (p.62).

Here are some examples of how other special children gave information, through observation, to begin their Visual Stimulation Programme. It is interesting to note that they *all* preferred very favourite humans to look at for visual stimulation.

CHILD	INFORMATION FROM CHILD	PLANNED PROGRAMME
A	Moves towards lights, especially windows.	Range of light stimulation, beginning in the Dark Room.
B	Follows slowly moving objects placed very close to face.	Developing of tracking in Dark Room, then shady box.
C	Doesn't do *anything* and fails to react to any visual stimulation.	Referral to orthoptist for visual assessment.
D	Eyes are continually rolling to the ceiling.	Behavioural attention programme to encourage 1:1 human looking.

E	Looks at objects if they are on child's left side.	All work placed on 'good' side.
F	Chooses *not* to look, only when the *child* wants.	'Promoted' to senior class of more able children to encourage looking and modelling of more acceptable social behaviour and 'looking'.
G	Uses his eyes to absorb everything around him because of his physical limitations	Provision of wide range of new visual experiences to explore.
H	Looks at what is in front of him, but does not track outside of his front vision.	Tracking programme, using sound linked to vision.
I	Sees everything but no further than the end of her nose.	Close work on tracking and fixating at face level, using face as 'desk'.
J	Eyes looking everywhere because of physical limitations, uses eyes to 'talk'.	Beginning of communication programme in conjunction with speech therapist.
K	Startles at a light being switched on/off.	Work on familiarising K with sudden lights.

OTHER PROFESSIONALS CAN HELP

Information should be requested from medical sources for all children who require visual assessment. This includes the child who 'appears' to see. An ophthalmic assessment will give information and details about actual defects, visual acuity, and visual field. The orthoptist can help with very specific ways of working with a child after the assessment, as well as carrying out regular assessments to ensure that there is no deterioration.

It is important to remember that some children can see, but cannot make sense of what they see, or otherwise use that vision.

Help can also be obtained from the Education Advisers from the RNIB, as well as from the specialist teachers for the visually handicapped within each county.

Other professionals, such as the physiotherapist or occupational therapist, can provide useful advice on careful positioning of the child for the most beneficial conditions relating to visual stimulation.

4   The Visual Stimulation and Preference Bank

WHAT IS A VISUAL STIMULATION BANK?

The Visual Stimulation Bank, including a Dark Room, is one part of a Sensory Bank. It is a resource to complement the Visual Stimulation Curriculum. The Visual Stimulation Bank is also used in conjunction with other areas of the child's programme, such as his or her attention programme or hand-reaching and grasping programme.

BEGINNING A VISUAL STIMULATION BANK

An area of the room should be designated as the learning space for visual stimulation. (The Dark Room space will also be designated as an extension of the visual stimulation space.) The factors of proper lighting and background should be taken into consideration when choosing the space. For example, it would be unwise to choose a corner with bright glare from windows, very prominent overhead lights, or very colourful pictures on the walls.

It is a good idea to have a suitable storage trolley or cupboard with appropriately sized trays or boxes to hold the separate visual stimulation units. The storage unit must be child-proof, in case an inquisitive visitor during the day muddles all the contents. Many of the units will also be stored in the Dark Room area, to be used there or borrowed for classroom use.

The visual stimulation should be divided into sections to suit *your* Visual Stimulation Curriculum.

SUGGESTED CONTENTS FOR A VISUAL STIMULATION AND
PREFERENCE BANK

It is a good idea to label each section, to allow easy access for the materials to be used for a particular session.

Main Visual Stimulation Sections

glitter	lights	fluorescent materials
shiny	mirrors	refractive
linked to sound	prisms	electrical
linked to touch	faces	garish colours
coloured lights	flashes	mechanical and moving
strobe		computer programs (graphics)

Some materials will be repeated in different sections. For example, the tinsel in a glitter box will also be in the jewellery box as a tinsel necklace or bracelet. The objective being set for the child will determine how the tinsel is used to meet the objective in each session.

Here are some visual stimulation materials that could be used in some of the mentioned visual stimulation sections.

Mirrors
concave
convex
flexible mirror
mirror mosaic
magnifying mirror
stand for mirror
full length sheet of foil on
   wall (*obtainable from
   science catalogues*)

Glitters
glitter body paint
glitter face make-up
glitter nail polish
tinsel
gold/silver material
gold gloves
assorted glittery necklaces
   and bracelets
foil Christmas decorations
gold papers
metallic papers
baubles
glitter paper

Coloured Lights
range of coloured bulbs to fit:
flexi-lamps
fairy lights
revolving disco lamps
twinkle disco tube
   (hi-speeds)
fibre-optic torch
night light
coloured lamps
disco hat with flashing
lights

Mechanical Objects
collection of cheap, bright,
gaudy mechanical animals,
cars, clocks, men, space
rockets, etc. which attract
by noise, movements, and
bright paints and
decorations. [*Ensure that
use of these objects is
supervised by an adult,
since many such toys are
not well built*]

Below are some suppliers of useful equipment:

Environmental Electrical Services, Manywells House, Many Wells Industrial Estate, Cullingworth, Bradford BD13 5DX.	A variety of lighting equipment suitable for use in a multisensory room.
Kirton Litework, Unit 2, Woodgate Park, Whitelund Estate, Morecambe LA3 3PS.	A wide range of visual stimulation equipment.
Tandy Corporation (*local branches*)	Cartwheel spinner lights, and high density strobe lights.
Paperchase, Mail Order Department, 213 Tottenham Court Road, London W1.	Vast range of papers and diffractives. Samples will be sent on request.
Rompa, Goyt Side Road, Chesterfield S40 2PH.	Solar projector, fibre-optic spray, tube light board, fibre-optic board, disco spot with colour wheel, star panel and winkle tube, revolving mirror ball.
Don't forget to try local shops.	For gay wrapping papers and diffractive materials, torches, and visual toys.

USING THE RESOURCES AND CURRICULUM WITH A CHILD

1 *Preparations beforehand*
   — Refer to the child's records for any medical condition before commencing any new area of the curriculum.
   — Make sure the child is wearing or using any required visual aids, as appropriate.
   — Send home and discuss the section on 'visual stimulation' in the Sensory Questionnaire.
   — Have someone else record reactions, if possible, to enable an objective recording to be taken.
   — Use a video camera for in-depth, freeze-frame analysis.
   — Decide the objective of the lesson beforehand, and keep to that objective.
   — Check that all materials are ready and available.

2   *The child in the visual stimulation area*
   — Talk to the child beforehand and let him know what is going to happen *before* you do anything.
   — Take the child to the visual stimulation area, explaining where you are going and what will happen.
   — Check that the positioning of the child is comfortable for both the child and for you.
   — Check the lighting—can the child see you?
   — Check that the recording materials or video camera are at hand. Do not record every session—eg. perhaps one out of five—but record any significant points in between.
   — Keep to the lesson objective.
   — Tell the child what visual stimulation material is going to be used and be very encouraging to him.
   — Use the visual stimulation material in a variety of positions.
   — Link the visual stimulation material with other sensory clues, if appropriate.
   — Allow time for the materials to have effect.
   — Repeat if appropriate. Observe and record while watching.
   — Tell the child when the visual stimulation session is finished and praise his co-operation or achievement.
   — Tell the child what is going to happen next and move him to the appropriate area.

3   *After the visual stimulation session*
   — Check recordings and plan the next step.
   — Repeat and repeat visual stimulation, even if there is no reaction—there may be one soon.
   — Let the family know what progress is being made and occasionally send home 'fun' homework.
   — Remember to include other people, who work with the child throughout the day, in the planning and execution of the Visual Stimulation Programme. They may have different approaches and ideas to contribute to the programme's value and success.
   — Most importantly, remember to GENERALISE the visual stimulation work in any new situation which might

arise. Talk to the child and remind him or point out the visual stimulation.

5 The Dark Room

WHAT IS A DARK ROOM?
The Dark Room is a specified area of the classroom or school, which is used to provide the best possible conditions for light stimulation with the very special child. The room or area is made as light-proof as possible by covering all external lighting and allowing only controlled lighting within. A wide range of materials is provided within the Dark Room to cover the whole area of the curriculum linked to stimulating a child's vision.

Space
The best Dark Room space is a small room within the classroom setting or school. It could be a disused stock cupboard, broom cupboard, or half of a room with dividers. This means that the Dark Room is permanent and can be fully developed. It also shows that the vision curriculum is seen as a very important part of the total curriculum, and that it is readily available to the rest of the school. Work in areas such as attention, tracking, and location can be undertaken in the Dark Room with the more able children in the school.

There are suitable alternatives to a room being used as a Dark Room. Here are four examples of alternative Dark Rooms:

1   A large shady cardboard box, big enough to contain seating for a child (see Fig. 2a). The end flaps of the box can be closed for maximum darkness. Visual stimulation, appropriate to the child, is hung or arranged within the box. Lights can be shone through holes made in the box.

2   A table covered with sheeting to provide a 'blanket tent'. There is a screen at one end of the table for visual stimulation materials.

3   A large box placed on a table for the child to look into for visual stimulation (see Fig. 2b). This is suitable for a child who can be positioned comfortably at a table.

Fig. 2a. A Dark Box made from a cardboard box packing case. Visual stimulation is provided within the box. Illustration by F.Moore.

4   A large box which can be used for a child who finds side-lying easier for viewing. Fig. 2c shows a child in a side-lying position using a pressure pad to work a light stimulation source. The child and box are covered with sheeting to obtain the maximum effect.

BEGINNING A DARK ROOM

An area of the classroom or a room should be designated as the learning space for vision stimulation. The area should be near SAFE electrical outlets. If an actual room is used, then sufficient outlets should be arranged to use the variety of lighting positioned around the room.

The Dark Room should also have adequate ventilation, or else the dark, enclosed space will become uncomfortable. A hot and bothered child will react to being hot and bothered, and not to the visual stimulation.

The comfortability of the Dark Room is also important. Comfortable seating and a comfortable floor covering enable both child and partner to work to their best potential.

It is helpful to have some low tables to hold the selection of permanent electrical equipment. The smaller visual materials can be stored in boxes beneath the tables for easy access. The boxes should be kept in the same positions in the room so that they can be easily located in the dark. The contents of the boxes should be regularly checked, especially for spent batteries, bulbs, etc.

It is advisable to hang a notice on the outside door of the Dark Room during a session to prevent a sudden influx of light should someone inadvertently enter.

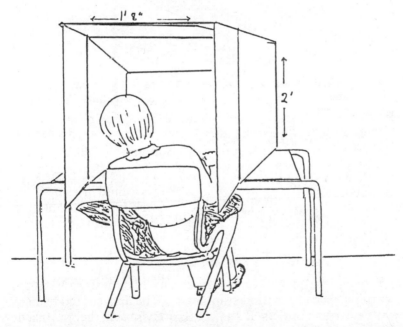

Fig. 2b. A large box is used to confine visual stimulation, as well as providing objects to touch and feel. Illustration by A. Stirzaker.

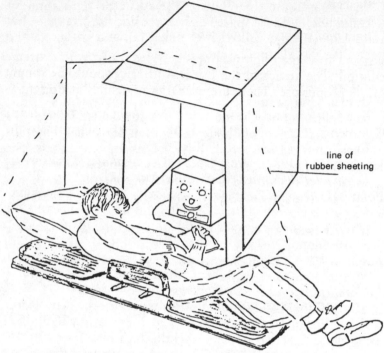

line of
rubber sheeting

Fig. 2c. A side-lying-board and box on the floor for easier vision. The back of the box may be opened for observation. Illustration by A. Stirzaker.

The walls, ceiling to floor, can be covered in a variety of reflective and glittery papers. There should also be plain black or white areas for projections of colour. Fairy lights and ornaments can be hung from a string which can be lowered like a washing line, from strong cup hooks fixed to the wall.

Each Dark Room will become unique, reflecting individual approaches.

ITEMS FOR USE IN THE DARK ROOM
Each tray of sections should be labelled to allow easy access and retrieval.

Main Dark Room Units

fluorescent	single beam	diffractive
shiny and glittery	electrical	strobe

flashers	coloured lights	faces
revolving lights	mirrors	prisms
light plus sound	light plus touch	

NOTE: Ultraviolet light should be used only with extreme caution. The advice of the Local Authority should be sought on its proper use. There are no DES guidelines at present.

The following articles on ultraviolet light may be of help:
Gumpelmayer, T. F. (1971). 'Is Black Light Harmful to the Eyes?', in *Lighting*, vol. 36, no. 3, pp 14-15.
Hughes, D. (1982). *Hazards of Occupational Exposure to Ultraviolet Radiation*. Science Reviews Ltd.
Poland, D. J., and Doebler, L. K. (1980). 'Effect of Blacklight Visual Field on Eye Contact Training of Spastic CP Children', in *Perceptual and Motor Skills*, vol. 51, no. 1, August, pp. 335-7.
Potenski, D. H. (1983). 'Use of Blacklight in Training Retarded Multiply Handicapped Deaf Blind Children', in *Journal of Visual Impairment and Blindness*, pp. 347-8.

Many of the visual stimulation materials for the Dark Room will be repeated in the main Visual Stimulation Bank. For example, diffractive paper may be in the prism section, the light-linked-to-touch and the glittery sections. The objective being set for the child would determine how the actual material was used.

Below are some visual stimulation materials that would be used in some of the mentioned Dark Room sections. Christmas time is the best buying time!

Coloured Lights
fairy lights
torch with coloured beams
variety of coloured light
  bulbs for use with angle
  poise lamps
slide projector very close
  to the wall for intense
  coloured image
torch with coloured
  attachable faces

Flashing Lights
revolving disco lamps
disco twinkle tube (*can be controlled in flashing rate*)
fairy lights with flasher
  control

Shiny/Glittery
tinsel
Christmas tree decorations
variety of glittery bracelets,
  rings, and necklaces
shiny metallic paper

USING THE DARK ROOM AND CURRICULUM WITH A CHILD
The use of the Dark Room follows a similar pattern to the advice in the section on using the main visual stimulation programme with the child. There are however, several points to add:

— Medical factors should be taken into consideration when planning light stimulation. A child who is prone to fits may have an adverse reaction to flickering or flashing lights. If there is a reaction, then that aspect should be terminated and other avenues explored.
— It is obviously very difficult to record in a Dark Room. It is only through working regularly with a child that any new observations will be seen, despite the darkness. The actual 'feel' of a child may give clues to his awareness of the visual stimulation being presented.
— Some children may show no reaction at all. This does not mean that they should not use the Dark Room. The work in the room should link strongly to the other senses to give them the clues they might need.
— Even if a child is totally blind, it is still appropriate to take him into the Dark Room with another child as a partner. The blind child cannot see the visual stimulation, but he can feel and experience other sensations in the room. The objectives for the child will not be visual, but in other sensory areas. The materials in the Dark Room are all linked to other senses.
— There should be an interval between each battery of stimulation presentations. Continued exposure without a break can lead to headaches.

Ideas for Use in a Dark Room
1 Reactions
   Use a multi-visual bombardment of lights and light

reflective materials to evoke a possible reaction.
Use: fairy lights
    large torch
    small torch
    strobe.
Use lights shone on:
    fluorescent paper
    tinfoil
    dark background
    bright colours
    textures.
Use lights in a variety of positions.
Use projections with slides.

2   Fixation/Attention
Use: steady light source and see if a child will fixate on
it.
Use: different lights
    different backgrounds for the lights.
Use: lights in variety of positions.

3   Tracking
See if the child will track a light beam. Hold head and move
to follow if necessary.
Go: up
    down
    across
    a wobbly line
    left to right
    right to left
    track quickly
    track slowly
    go across midline.
Use: a random line.
Use: a circle.

4   Choppy Tracking
Use: lights blinked on and off along a line.
Use: horizontal
    vertical
    oblique
    circular lines.

Use: cardboard with half inch holes along a line, move light behind.

5   Link with Other Senses
Use: a light source in conjunction with another sense, eg. sound.
Use: vibrating pillow when light is on
bell sounds when light is on
perfume when light is on
tambourine when light is on
soft tactile stimulation when light is on.

6   Awareness of Light On/Off
Present a light source and block it.
Use decreasing size of object blocking the light—allow child to remove it if possible (could be tactile sensation by using a soft/hard material to block).

7   Decrease in Background Light
Use a light with less intensity if child is able to distinguish shapes, etc. Go out of dark room and use other areas.
Use: natural light
a corridor
the hall
a cupboard.

6   A Partial Visual Stimulation Programme for a Child with Profound Learning Difficulties and Little Sight
Courtesy of Anita Royall

Alice's Present Level
Regards objects presented at eye level. Brings her hands to her mouth, attempts to feel objects which come into contact with her hands and tries to bring them to her mouth.

Objective
For Alice to regard her hands close to her face.
1   Regards adult hands on hers with light shining on them in Dark Room.
2   Regards own hands with light on them with physical prompt in Dark Room.
3   Regards own hands with light on them without prompt in Dark Room.

4 Regards own hands with bright light on them in classroom.
5 Regards hands with glitter gloves on them with prompt (no light).
6 Regards hands with glitter gloves without prompt.
7 Regards own hands with physical prompt.
8 Regards own hands voluntarily.

Long-term aim: for Alice to use her hands to play.
Objective: for Alice to regard her hands.

PROGRAMME

Cognitive (visual)	Motor (position)
Dark Room	
1 In co-active situation with adult holding Alice's hands in playing position in front of her eyes. Broad light beam to allow her to see her arms and hands.	Sitting cross-legged, back to adult, hips back, head midline.
2 Removal of physical prompts gradually, repeat above on Alice's supported hands and arms.	As above.
3 Broad beam light as before but Alice in side-lying position to encourage voluntary movement of hands without prompting.	Side-lying—right side is best for Alice.

Classroom (1:1 situation)
For Awareness of Hands
Materials
vibrating toys
cymbals
guitar.

In co-active situation, hands to hands with adult, gradual removal of physical prompts.	Sitting back to adult at first. Later in Rifton chair.

Hand and finger songs and
rhymes.

*To Encourage Regard of
Hands*

Glitter gloves on Alice's hands, adult holding Alice's hands in front of her eyes, increase and decrease distance from her face.	Side-lying. Encourage extension and flexion of arms to bring hands up to eye level. Prompt her to use natural movements instead of spasms.

When left on her own, Alice to be placed side-lying in fixation area—mobiles hanging in front of her face and near to her hands so even involuntary movements make her aware of these.

Mobiles to Be Used
Cascade of small gold bells. Tinsel mobile. Wooden faces mobile. Light to be shone on these at first, remove eventually.
    Use of video to observe Alice in solitary situations.
    Mother has a copy of this programme and has agreed to help at home by helping Alice to become aware of her hands when caring for her, and by playing hand games such as pat-a-cake, round and round the garden, etc., at eye level near to her face.

Observations from November 1983 to December 1984

Date	:	3 November 1983
Materials	:	Broad beam of light shone onto hands 4″ from face.
Situation	:	Co-active with me sitting cross-legged, back to me, head mid-line. Light shone onto hands.
Exposure Total	:	Five minutes.
Response	:	Lifted head and turned towards light, smiled, cooed. When light moved away, stopped smiling and vocalising.
Objective Response	:	Looked at light rather than hands at first. When I touched her nose with her hands, her eyes turned inwards, looked at her fingers, and smiled.

Date   : 10 November 1983
Materials   : Broad beam of light flashed back and forth, then
               flashed light on adult's fingers, and wriggled them.
Situatioh   : Dark Room, sitting between adult's legs,
               propped up by left leg.
Exposure   : Three minutes.
Total
Response   : Lifted head up from dropped position,
               stretched legs.
Objective
Response   : Looked at light at first, but when adult's fingers
               in front of light and wriggled, her eyes followed
               movement, she smiled, and made an 'ahh' sound.

Date   : 11 November 1983
Materials   : Broad beam of light directed first onto adult's
               face, then onto hands (adult's).
Situation   : Dark Room, propped up facing adult.
Exposure   : Three minutes.
Total
Response   : Cooed and smiled, lifted head but appeared at
               first to be watching coloured paper on wall.
Objective
Response   : Did not appear to be actually regarding hands
               and fingers.

Date   : 16 November 1983
Materials   : Glitter gloves on Alice's hands. Tinsel wrapped
               around adult's hands.
Situation   : Music therapy room. Sitting between adult's
               legs for hand movement session.
Exposure   : Thirty-minute session. Ten minutes for hands
               and arms.
Total
Response   : This session is to provide a multisensory
               experience which Alice enjoys. She usually
               looks towards the sound of the adult's voice
               and smiles and coos.
Objective
Response   : Turned head towards hands, eyes turned in-
               wards, when hands near nose.

Date   : 5 January 1984
Materials   : Hanging bell mobile. Normal classroom light.
Situation   : Alice lying on right side, back to light in class-
               room, underneath hanging bell mobile (tinsel
               wrapped around string). Glitter wrapped around
               her hands.
Exposure   : Ten minutes.
Total
Response   : Stretched legs, eyes converged, smiled, cooed.
Objective
Response   : Whole left arm moved in upwards circular
               movement; when hand came in contact with
               bells, she laughed at the sound they made. I
               placed the bells into her hand, she brought them
               towards her face and smiled and vocalised, left
               eye moved towards her hand.

Date   : 9 January 1984
Materials   : Pencil torch placed in left clenched hand and
               held to the side of her left eye (hand glowed red).
Situation   : Dark Room, propped up on cushion facing
               me.
Exposure   : Four minutes.
Total
Response   : Arched back, straightened legs, then brought
               head forward, tongue came out.
Objective
Response   : Eyes turned towards her hand, she smiled. I
               moved her hand across her face and touched
               her nose; her eyes followed the movement, she
               laughed.

Date   : 12 January 1984
Materials   : Felt doll (red and yellow). Christmas garland.
               Glitter doll wrapped around her left hand.
Situation   : In messy area and classroom.
Exposure   : Five minutes.
Total
Response   : Less response to visual stimulation than usual.
               Seemed to respond to adult's voice and touch
               instead.

Objective
Response : Appeared to be following doll for a few seconds. Tired rapidly.

Date : 13 January 1984
Materials : Spot light. Glitter gloves.
Situation : In front of mirror, between adult's legs.
Exposure : Six minutes.
Total
Response : Watched the light. Smiled and cooed when adult's face close to hers.

Objective
Response : Brought hands to her mouth. Did not look at hands.

Date : 16 January 1984
Materials : Pencil torch placed in Alice's hand, her fingers closed around it. This gave a red glow to her clenched fist.
Situation : Fixation area, lights out. Alice's back to window.
Exposure : Six minutes.
Total
Response : (No entry.)
Objective
Response : I moved her hands towards her nose from the left side, 6" from her face; followed with left eye, smiled when 3" from her face, cooed when her hand touched her nose. I repeated this with just my finger in her hands. No response shown this time.

Date : 16 January 1984
Materials : Three small concave mirrors hanging in front of Alice, with broad beam of light shone on them from behind her. The warmth from the light caused the mirrors to move, with their light playing on Alice's face.
Situation : Fixation area. Alice lying on her right side, on her own.
Exposure : Ten minutes.

Total
Response : Eyes widened and moved horizontally and vertically to the light movements. Moved her head, smiled, and cooed.

Objective
Response : Used left hand to knock against mirror. This caused her to smile, but she was watching the movements of the mirrors, not her hands. Brought the right hand (which was lying on the floor) to her mouth. Left hand again knocked against the mirror and she moved her head and eyes to watch light pattern.

Date : 19 January 1984
Materials : Large pieces of foil paper: silver in right hand, red in left hand.
Situation : Classroom. Natural light. Alice in her own chair, back to window. Other active children working around and around her.
Exposure : Thirty minutes.
Total
Response : Smiled and cooed. Stretched legs, put head down to hand, thrust out tongue and mouthed the paper in her right hand.

Objective
Response : Bent head and looked at red paper in her left hand, smiled and cooed. Head up again, brought left hand round towards left eye, looked at paper, smiled and made 'ahhh' sound.

Date : 19 January 1984
Materials : Large pieces of shiny paper as above, but torch shone on hands.
Situation : In Dark Room. Sitting supported. No sounds. Torch shone on hands individually.
Exposure : Ten minutes.
Total
Response : Moved whole body at first. Stretched legs, moved head back, then stilled and started to move her hands.

Objective
Response : Turned eyes towards left hand, brought towards face, cooed and laughed, opened mouth, thrust out tongue and licked paper, then moved hand up to her left eye. Torch then shone on right hand, brought right hand to right eye and left it there while left hand took red paper to and from mouth.

Date : 26 January 1984
Materials : Small tin with shiny lid in her left hand. Small strawberry smell-soap in her right hand.
Situation : In her chair, in classroom, back to window, normal light.
Exposure : Fifteen minutes.
Total
Response : Moved head, it flopped down near to her left hand, eyes moved towards hand, smiled.

Objective
Response : Brought both hands over her face, cooed, smiled, thrust out tongue. Left hand went down, then back to her face.

Date : 26 January 1984
Materials : Small piece of silver card tied around her wrist and placed behind thumb and between fingers on left hand.
Situation : Sitting in her chair, small hall, dull light.
Exposure : Six minutes.
Total
Response : Stilled at first, then smiled.
Objective
Response : Brought hand to face, smiled, cooed, thrust tongue out, hand down, then up again, cooed, mouthed card.

Date : 2 February 1984
Materials : Large fluorescent poppet beads placed near to left hand.
Situation : On side-lying board in messy area (only one small window in this area) back to light.

Exposure : Fifteen minutes.
Total
Response : Stretched legs, moved head near to beads. Smiled, cooed, thrust out tongue and mouthed.

Objective
Response : Moved clenched hands up to mouth, then away from mouth and left hand touched head and opened out, looked at beads and smiled.

Date : 7 February 1984
Materials : Fibre-optic torch enclosed in her left hand to give red glow. Multi-coloured fibres touching her right hand.
Situation : Dark Room, supported by cushions, facing adult.
Exposure : Five minutes.
Total
Response : Turned head towards hands, smiled, laughed, cooed.

Objective
Response : Eyes looked towards her hands, vocalised, and brought her left hand to her mouth.

Date : 8 February 1984
Materials : Cascade of gold bells.
Situation : Lying on her right side in fixation and tracking area. Normal classroom light. Alice with back to window, left on her own.
Exposure : Ten minutes.
Total
Response : Put head back and looked at bells, legs stretched, thrust out tongue, moved left arm in circular movement and knocked bells, laughed at sound.

Objective
Response : When hand knocked bells, fingers opened, she looked in direction of her hand and bells, and smiled and vocalised.

Date : 9 February 1984
Materials : Silver paper in left hand. Red shiny paper in right hand. Red shiny paper suspended over right shoulder, silver over left shoulder.

Situation : Sitting in her chair in large cardboard box in a north-facing classroom. Natural subdued light. (These notes taken from video recording.)

Exposure : Thirty minutes.

Total
Response : Calling out 'oooh' with big smiles. Right leg lifting on and off block. Brought hands midline across her chest, head back. Right hand lifted silver paper and knocked suspended red paper, looked and laughed at resulting movement. Head back to midline, stilled, turned left eye to suspended silver paper, turned head to right in in order to use left eye, probably for preference for red. Opened mouth, thrust out tongue, lifted head and cooed, appeared to listen to crackle of paper.

Objective
Response (No entry.)

Date : 9 February 1984

Materials : Small silver card in left hand. Diffractive paper Mickey Mouse in right hand.

Situation : Continuation of previous situation, without suspended stimuli.

Exposure : Continuation of previous situation, without suspended stimuli.

Total
Response : Looked for suspended stimulus, right hand moved upwards as though trying to knock. Appeared to catch sight of diffractive material and smiled, looked upwards again and around the box. Lifted left hand up, caught sight of silver card in left hand, eyes looked upwards again to right where red paper was previously suspended. Continually looking up with head until an involuntary head movement caused her to catch sight of silver card in her left hand, head went back, stilled, head down and she voluntarily brought her hand to within 3" of her left eye, smiled and laughed, mouth opened, took

her hand to her mouth. No longer searched for suspended items, head kept down now. Brought card towards mouth and 'talked' to it. Caught sight of diffractive item in right hand, left eye appeared to look at it, smiled, brought right hand to left eye and smiled and laughed. Brought hands together at midline and laughed, stilled and put head back when other children entered the room. Head down again, looked at diffractive material in right hand, lots of mouth and tongue movement. These movements repeated.

Date	:	December 1984
Materials	:	Mirror, 4" from her face.
Situation	:	In Dark Room. On poly bag, supported by adult's arm behind her shoulders, to help head control and arm movement. Small torch shone from right side.
Exposure	:	(No entry.)
Reactions	:	Eyes widened, then converged, then looked straight ahead. She made *no* attempt to turn towards the light. She looked at the mirror image, she smiled, 'cooed', 'ahhhhed,' put her tongue out to touch mirror. Arms and hands moved inwards, she laughed.

When she looked at my face in the mirror, or my face close to her, she smiled, but this was the only reaction.

Date	:	December 1984
Materials	:	Cascade of foil strips hanging from a screen, mobile of shiny objects, including a blown-up silver lining from a wine box, with red cellophane streamers hanging from it, and a diffractive star.
Situation	:	Alice lying on side, in classroom, dark covered screen blocks light from the window and foil strips hang from screen.
Exposure	:	(No entry.)
Reactions	:	At first, we used the blower from a fan heater to move the streamers and mobiles to attract her

attention. She smiled at these and vocalised and tried to touch them with her hands and mouth. She eventually managed this, so, after three weeks, we removed the fan.

She continued to look at them and touch them. After a further two weeks, she started to grasp the foil streamers in her hands and turn over and take them with her, wrapping them around her body. She smiles and vocalises when this happens. If we move her with her back to the stimuli, she turns back towards them and grasps again.

She now anticipates where she is going when we carry her over to that area of the classroom in the morning. She starts to smile and coo as soon as I move in that direction. This does *not* happen when she is taken to other areas of the classroom.

7 **Visual Stimulation and Preference—Action Check List**
1 Read relevant books and articles. See relevant films.
2 Visit other schools and review their visual stimulation banks and curricula.
3 Begin collecting visual stimulation materials to equip your Bank and Dark Room.
4 Plan a Visual Stimulation Curriculum with main aims, goals, and units.
5 Plan a recording system.
6 Involve parents and other people important to the child.
7 Plan and equip the Visual Stimulation Bank and Dark Room.
8 Keep materials up to date and keep adding new materials to the Bank and Room.
9 Evaluate the Visual Stimulation Curriculum, Bank, and Dark Room regularly.

8 **Helpful Books, Articles, and Societies**
Please refer to the main bibliography in Chapter 1 for general information that will help in developing a sensory curriculum and also help with recording and assessment.

Dale, J. (1977). *Progress Guide for Deaf/Blind and for Severely Handicapped Children.* Obtainable from: SENSE, 311 Grays Inn Road, London WC1X 8PT.

Department of Education and Science. *Lighting and Acoustic Criteria for the Visually Handicapped and Hearing Impaired in Schools,* Design Note 2.

Eden, J. (1978). *The Eye Book.* Harmondsworth: Penguin Books.

Fraiberg, S. (1977). *Insights from the Blind.* London: Souvenir Press.

Freeman, P. (1975). *Understanding the Deaf Blind Child.* London: Heinemann Medical Books.

Royal National Institute for the Blind. *Guidelines for Teachers and Parents of Visually Handicapped Children with Additional Handicaps.* Obtainable from: RNIB, 224 Great Portland Street, London W1N 6AA.

Halle, B. (1976). *Motor Development in Children: Normal and Retarded.* (Chapter on sight.) Oxford: Blackwell Scientific Publications.

Jose, R. T., Smith, A. J., and Shane, G. S. (1980). 'Evaluating and Stimulating Vision in the Multiply Impaired', in *Journal of Visual Impairment and Blindness*, January 1980, pp. 2-8 (ideas for dark rooms).

Kiernan, C. *et al.* (1978). *Starting Off.* (Chapter 7 on sight.) London: Souvenir Press.

Kiernan, C., and Jones, M. (1982). *Behaviour Assessment Battery.* (Sections on visual-motor inspection and tracking.) Windsor: NFER–Nelson.

Langley, M.B. (1976). 'Functional Vision Screening for Severely Handicapped Children', from *New Outlook for the Blind*, October 1976.

McInnes, J. M., and Treffry, J. A. (1982). *Deaf Blind Infants and Children.* Milton Keynes: Open University Press. (This book is comprehensive and excellent.)

Newson, E., and Hipgrave, T. (1982). *Getting Through to Your Handicapped Child.* Chapter 7, section on 'Looking'. Cambridge University Press.

Programme Planner for Blind and Partially Sighted Children of Low Ability Including ESN(S). Obtainable from: Peripatetic Service for Visually Handicapped Children, Shawgrove

School, Cavendish Road, West Didsbury, Manchester.
Royal National Institute for the Blind. *Information Exchange—* Very informative publication full of new ideas and articles especially for the visually impaired very special person. Details from: RNIB, 224 Great Portland Street, London W1N 6AA.
Rennie, M., and Taylor, H. S. (1980). 'Assessing the Visual Abilities of Multiply Impaired Blind Children', from *Insight*, vol. 2, no. 2.
Reynell-Zinkin Development Scales for Young Visually Handicapped Children. Obtainable from NFER–Nelson (via your speech therapist).
Sheridan, M. D. (1976). *Stycar Vision Test.* Windsor: NFER–Nelson.
Simon, G. B. (1981). *Next Step on the Ladder.* Section 1, use of sight and hearing. Obtainable from British Institute of Mental Handicap, Kidderminster, Worcs.

HELPFUL SOCIETIES
SENSE. *Family Centre:* 86, Cleveland Road, Ealing, London W13. *Headquarters:* 11-13 Clifton Terrace, Finsbury Park, London N4 3SR.
Research Centre for the Education of the Visually Handicapped, Selby Wick House, 59 Selby Wick Road, Birmingham B29.
Royal National Institute for the Blind, 224 Great Portland Street, London W1N 6AA.

3 DEVELOPING A TASTE CURRICULUM AND TASTE BANK

Contents

1 Introduction

WHY A TASTE CURRICULUM?

The sense of taste is categorised into salt, sweet, bitter, and sour. Taste is perceived via the taste buds on the tongue. Children's taste buds are much more widely distributed within the mouth than are adults'. Thousands of taste buds are scattered over the surface of the tongue, but children also have them on the inside of the cheeks.

Developing a tolerance for a range of tastes is very important to the special needs child. Difficulties can arise when a child will accept only a limited range of tastes in a limited range of foods. This can lead to dietary deficiencies and bowel problems.

Slow and unresponsive eating habits may be due to a child's narrow range of tastes. The child may also feed without pleasure and with indifference to the foods presented.

There may be problems at home, because, as well as the main family meal, a special meal must be made for the child.

A child may have difficulty in using the mouth and tongue for communication because these organs have not been sufficiently stimulated by normal tasting and feeding actions.

A Taste Curriculum, linked to a Taste Bank, can help to develop the sense of taste as fully as possible. This will hopefully lead to a wider and more varied diet, and hence to one that is better balanced and more nutritious.

The Taste Curriculum can also help in motivating a child to respond more positively to feeding by actively promoting the development of likes, and dislikes, to various tastes. Based on the taste of a particular food, the brain recalls other impressions by smell, visual, textural, and environmental appeal. In other words, the child is awakened to new taste experiences and is permitted to show his or her own preferences for tastes.

THE LINK TO A CHILD'S FEEDING PROGRAMME
The Taste Curriculum and Taste Bank should complement and extend a child's individual feeding programme in the areas of taste, temperature, texture and consistency.

Help with the main feeding programme should come from other professionals, such as the speech therapist, the occupational therapist and the physiotherapist. These specialists can help in such practical areas as comfortable positioning, appropriate utensils, control of head, tongue and mouth, and in planning individual feeding programmes.

If these professionals are *not* available, then steps should be taken by the Headteacher to ensure that these necessary resources *are* made available to all teachers, when and as needed.

At the end of this chapter is a list of reading material useful in planning feeding programmes.

THE LINK TO SMELL

Taste and smell are closely related. The sense of smell aids the taste buds in the mouth to help a person appreciate flavour and taste to the fullest extent possible. You may not be aware of smelling your food and drink, but the odours reach the brain from the back of the mouth, as well as via the nose.

If a child is given the opportunity to smell before tasting, then the brain has the opportunity to blend the two messages together to enhance the taste. Therefore, the child's Smell Programme should be closely co-ordinated with the Taste and Feeding Programmes, rather than independently.

2   Planning a Taste Curriculum

SETTING YOUR AIMS

The main aim for the Taste Curriculum should be to enlarge the child's range and awareness of tastes, ultimately yielding the fullest benefit to the child through improved feeding.

SETTING YOUR GOALS

The goals that are set for the Taste Curriculum should not be seen as graduated steps. There cannot be a set of developmental goals which vary more widely from person to person than in the area of taste.

Everyone has very personalised tastes and levels of taste, including the special child. The goals that are set for a special child must not be set in isolation, but rather must be interlinked to other areas of the curriculum. For example, the goal of 'beginning a controlled range of mouth movements' should relate strongly to the child's Communication Programme, as well as to the child's development of hand-to-mouth movements.

The following list includes some of the main goals in planning a taste curriculum:

— toleration and enjoyment of tastes,
— stimulation and awareness of tastes,
— increased awareness of tastes linked to smell,
— acceptance of different flavours,

— improved feeding,
— desensitisation of the face and mouth,
— beginning of a controlled range of mouth movements,
— beginning of a controlled range of tongue movements,
— increased body movement,
— beginning of vocalisation,
— simple discrimination of tastes,
— beginning of a taste memory, i.e. remembering and recognising tastes.

One or more main goals would be selected from this list, for a particular child, to be included with other areas of priority in the total planned curriculum for that child.

PLANNING TASTE UNITS

The main areas in which to begin a Taste Programme are with *sweet and savoury* tastes. As the curriculum develops, these main areas can be broken down into more precise units. For example, the savoury area could include sour, bitter, salty, spiced, and herbal units.

Examples of curricula for the two areas, sweet and savoury, are shown below.

CURRICULUM DATA
Savoury Tastes

Curriculum area : Cognitive
Main objective : Sensory development
Stage : Tastes—savoury
Resources : School curriculum, speech therapist

1 Accepts all tastes with indifference.
2 Accepts strong savoury tastes.
3 Rejects strong savoury tastes.
4 Accepts mild savoury tastes.
5 Rejects mild savoury tastes.
6 Accepts savoury food mixed with familiar food.
7 Discriminates between savoury tastes.
8 Shows preference for certain savoury tastes.
9 Other.

CURRICULUM DATA
Sweet Tastes

Curriculum area	:	Cognitive
Main objective	:	Sensory development
Stage	:	Tastes—sweet
Resources	:	School curriculum, speech therapist

1 Accepts all tastes with indifference.
2 Accepts very sweet tastes.
3 Rejects very sweet tastes.
4 Accepts mild sweet tastes.
5 Rejects mild sweet tastes.
6 Accepts sweet tastes mixed with familiar food.
7 Discriminates between sweet tastes.
8 Shows preference for certain sweet tastes.
9 Other.

TASTE RANGE, CONSISTENCY, TEXTURE AND TEMPERATURE

There are other units to include in the Taste Curriculum, as well as the *range* of taste stimulation, which link closely to a child's feeding programme. These units are texture, consistency and temperature.

The following examples illustrate how these units can be combined in the programme.

Taste Range	Consistency	Texture	Temperature
banana	puréed banana	chopped banana	banana ice lolly
apple	apple drink	apple slice	baked apple
orange	mandarin segments	orange flavour wafer	orange whip
meat	gravy	barbeque crisps	hot Oxo drink

Curriculum units for temperature, consistency and texture are shown in the examples on the following pages.

CURRICULUM DATA
Temperature

Curriculum area	:	Cognitive
Main objective	:	Sensory development
Stage	:	Taste—temperature
Resources	:	School curriculum, speech therapist

1   Is indifferent to a variety of food temperatures presented.
2   Takes warm foods.
3   Takes foods at room temperature.
4   Takes chilled foods.
5   Takes cold foods.
6   Takes frozen foods.
7   Takes food with a mixture of temperatures in a meal.
8   Shows preference for foods at certain temperatures.
9   Other.

CURRICULUM DATA
Texture and Consistency

Curriculum area   :   Cognitive
Main objective   :   Sensory development
Stage   :   Taste—texture and consistency
Resources   :   School curriculum, speech therapist

1   Takes dummy dipped in semi-solid food.
2   Takes thick, puréed food.
3   Takes thickened food.
4   Takes thinned, puréed food.
5   Takes thinned drink.
6   Takes selection of textures that melt in the mouth.
7   Takes finely mashed food.
8   Takes roughly mashed food.
9   Takes roughly mashed, chopped, or grated food.
10   Takes coarsely chopped food.
11   Takes a selection of chopped and mashed foods.
12   Takes small pieces of soft food.
13   Takes mouth-size pieces of soft food.
14   Takes small pieces of chewy food.
15   Takes mouth-size pieces of chewy food.
16   Other.

3   Linking the Child to the Taste Curriculum

THE FAMILY CAN HELP
Most feeding and tasting experiences occur at home or in other
caring environments. Information provided from the home is a

good basis on which to begin building a Taste Programme for the child and for setting realistic goals.

A simple sensory questionnaire should be completed by the family so that they are involved in the Taste Programme at home, as well as at school. (See Appendix A for a sample Sensory Questionnaire.)·

A Parent Workshop in the sensory area of taste will help explain the aims of this particular area and further involve the family. 'Taste' homework can occasionally be sent home for the child. (See Appendix B for a sample Homework Record.)

Families usually rise to the challenge—especially siblings. One month, homework could be a request for a range of onion-flavoured foods to be experienced. Another month, it could be for sticky foods to be placed around the mouth (in order to make the tongue reach to find them).

THE SCHOOL CAN HELP

Information at school can be collected using a simple recording form. (See Appendix C for a sample of Simple Record Keeping.) This form should be kept for a given period of time, during which a range of tastes are presented to a child. The form will provide on-going information on the child's progress in this area of the sensory curriculum.

There is a range of reactions and non-reactions to be observed and used as the first steps in an individual Taste Progamme.

The following example lists some of the ranges of taste reactions which you may observe in a Taste Recording. Remember, some children may look as though they are rejecting a taste when they are actually enjoying it. Only *your* close association with the child will help you to identify the true reaction.

CURRICULUM DATA
Rejection of Tastes

Curriculum area : Cognitive
Main objective   : Sensory development
Stage   : Taste—rejection
Resources   : School curriculum, speech therapist

LOCATION OF TASTE

1   Rejects taste on: lips
                                tongue
                                side of mouth
                                back of mouth

RANGE OF REACTIONS

1   Startles.
2   Moves away from the taste.
3   Widens eyes.
4   Shudders.
5   Opens mouth wide.
6   Moves tongue.
7   Moves teeth.
8   Closes mouth.
9   Grimaces.
10   Moves head.
11   Moves body.
12   Spits out.
13   Pushes out with tongue.
14   Pushes out with teeth.
15   Over-salivates.
16   Other.

CURRICULUM DATA

Acceptance of Tastes

Curriculum area   :   Cognitive
Main objective   :   Sensory development
Stage   :   Taste—acceptance
Resources   :   School curriculum, speech therapist

LOCATION OF TASTE

1   Accepts taste on: lips
                                 tongue
                                 side of mouth
                                 back of mouth

RANGE OF REACTIONS

1 Moves towards the taste.
2 Moves head.
3 Moves lips.
4 Moves tongue.
5 Moves mouth.
6 Moves tongue against teeth.
7 Moves tongue around inside mouth.
8 Moves tongue outside mouth.
9 Swallows.
10 Produces saliva.
11 Facial expression changes.
12 Gurgles.
13 Licks lips.
14 Other.

THE CHILD CAN HELP

The child 'helps' directly by exhibiting reactions and responses to the stimuli presented, which the teacher observes during each tasting session. The observations made during tasting sessions with an individual child provide the foundation for constructing the particular Taste Programme for that child. The resulting programme should be designed specifically for that child and should meet that child's particular needs. In other words, a general Taste Curriculum cannot be applied universally to all children—each child is unique.

To show how a child provides the information which forms the basis for an individual Taste Programme, the following example illustrates a typical recording of a child's reactions to tastes. The example shown was derived from a complete set of recordings taken over a period of one month. The recordings were used to establish the main taste objectives for the child. These objectives were 'to increase response to a range of sticky foods both inside and outside the mouth' and 'exposure to a range of salty foods'.

RECORDING FORM

Sensory Area: Taste   Name: George

Materials	Date	Exposure	Response	Comments
1) crunchy peanut butter		One taste.	Needed to be persuaded to open mouth. —then accepted. —seemed to enjoy. —closed lips together and brought them into mouth.	On my lap before lunch. Placed on tongue and lips.
2) salt		Few grains sprinkled on tongue	No reaction, just accepted with eyes half-closed.	On my lap.
3) sultanas		Four sultanas placed in mouth.	Shuddered. Gagged. Used tongue to try to push sultanas out of mouth. Grimaced.	On my lap. Placed in mouth.
4) Bournvita		One-quarter teaspoon.	Took into side of mouth —accepted. —lips closed. —smacked lips. —brought grains from lips into mouth.	On polyblob.

OTHER PROFESSIONALS CAN HELP

Information should be requested from other professionals to help in planning a Taste Programme. The multi-disciplinary approach is of great importance. The speech therapist, occupational therapist, physiotherapist and dietician can all contribute in establishing a child's individual Taste Programme and help in executing that programme.

The dinner lady, who helps feed the child each day, can also provide useful insights into a child's taste patterns, and should be included as part of the multi-disciplinary planning team.

Example Case Study of a Taste Programme
The following is an example of an actual Taste Programme developed for a two-year-old child (Colin) who had been tube-fed since birth.

Long-term aim: For Colin to take a variety of food.
Objective: For Colin to take food by mouth, linked to communication.
Professionals involved: Teacher, nursery nurses, speech therapist, occupational therapist, physiotherapist, orthoptist, teacher for hearing impaired, paediatrician.

The orthoptist's report showed that Colin was using both eyes together. He frequently rolled his eyes upwards. This information was required to know his visual field before showing him his food, spoon, etc.

Colin's hearing report showed that he responded to and reacted appropriately to simple commands when wearing his hearing aids. The teacher for the hearing impaired visited him at school and at home.

The physiotherapist and occupational therapist both gave advice on gross motor and self-help skills, and aids regarding seating.

The paediatrician reported that there were no medical problems to prevent Colin from commencing with the Taste Programme.

The speech therapist gave advice on mouth and tongue control for the encouragement of swallowing. Use of simple Makaton sign language was started both at home and at school.

An outline of the Taste Programme for Colin, and results after five months, are given below.

Taste Programme for Colin

Cognitive Areas	Motor Areas
For awareness of mouth: games such as blowing raspberries, sticking out his tongue, 'Indian calls', puffing out cheeks, and popping cheeks, etc.	Programme to encourage mobility, to allow Colin to explore, was prepared with assistance of the occupational therapist and the physiotherapist.

For hand awareness:
hand and finger rhymes
and songs, messy play,
musical instruments, social
participation in games with
other children.

For awareness of food and
feeding:
symbolic play with cups,
spoons, dish, jug, etc.;
encouraging Colin to give
sweets, etc., to other
children in the class.

Sensory stimulation:
to promote awareness of
smell, food smells, eg.
chocolate, peppermint,
marmite, etc., linked to
feeding by offering very
small tastes.

Manipulates toys to
encourage use of hands.
Ladder-back chairs to help
Colin pull himself to
standing position.
Cell Barnes walker and
Rifton Chair.

Progress Summary with the Taste Programme
We started the actual feeding by spoon feeding the tube
formula. Colin objected strongly at first, but accepted
eventually. The liquid was then thickened with Ready Brek
cereal and placed in the side of the mouth, behind his teeth.
After some objection, we managed to get six spoonfuls into his
mouth, some of which stayed in. Colin sucked his hand at the
same time, so we encouraged him to put his hands into the food
dish.

The next step was to introduce instant whip and blancmange
into the feeding scheme. He rejected the instant whip, which
was given cold, but accepted the warm blancmange.

Colin now takes about six ounces of warm, smooth-textured
food without objection. He responds to commands such as
'Open your mouth' and 'Look here', and tries to imitate the
Makaton sign for 'good boy'. He sucks food off the spoon and
has put a spoon towards his mouth. He will accept chocolate

drops and tastes of sweet foods, such as honey and jam. He tries to put food into other children's mouths.

Since taking solid food and becoming more aware of his mouth Colin makes more sounds and uses his voice to attract attention.

4   The Taste Bank

WHAT IS A TASTE BANK?

The Taste Bank is one part of a Sensory Bank. It is a resource to complement the Taste Curriculum. The Taste Bank should present a wide, stimulating range of taste experiences. The Bank is also used in conjunction with a child's Feeding Programme and should be linked closely with the child's Smell Programme.

BEGINNING A TASTE BANK

An area of the room should be designated as the learning space for taste. The canteen area, or home economics area, could be used for taste sessions, as appropriate. It should be near the smell area.

It is wise to have a suitable storage trolley or cupboard, with appropriately sized trays or boxes, to contain the separate taste units. The storage space must be child-proof, just in case! A good idea is to reverse a trolley or storage unit when not in use.

The items for tasting should be kept in clean, covered containers, with a supply of clean spoons and spatulas. Expiry dates and the condition of taste items should be regularly checked. New taste items should be added to the stock as required.

The taste items should be divided into sections to suit *your* Taste Curriculum. In the next section are some suggested taste areas.

SUGGESTIONS FOR SECTIONS IN A TASTE BANK

It is a good idea to label each section to allow easy access for the particular tastes to be used in a session.

1   Main Taste Sections
    salt   sweet   sour   bitter

2 Subsidiary Taste Sections
   fruity   fiery   spicy   bland   herbal
   savoury   dried fruits

3 Subsidiary Consistency and Texture Sections
   melting   sticky   creamy   liquid   fizzy
   fine   coarse   lumpy
   thick-   thin-consistency

Some taste items will be repeated in different taste and consistency sections. For example, a chocolate flake could be used in the sweet section, the melting section, and the coarse consistency section. The main taste objectives set for the child will determine how the chocolate flake is used to meet the objective in each tasting session.

Some of the taste items which could be used in the example sections are as follows:

Sticky, sweet section
chocolate spread
peanut butter
honey
Angel Whip
jams
nut spread
yoghurt

Melting section
sorbets
ice cream
ice lolly
sugar strands
syrup
Flying Saucers
rice paper
chocolate flake
meringue
fudge

Strong savoury tastes
(minute tastes)
Ploughman's Pickle
tomato sauce
brown sauce
soya sauce
mixed spice
mustard
piccalilli
cheese spread

Fiery tastes
(minute tastes)
peppermint
curry powders
hot spices
hot pickles
Worcestershire sauce
brandy flavouring

USING THE TASTE BANK AND CURRICULUM WITH A CHILD

1 *Preparations beforehand*
   — Refer to the child's records for any medical condition, allergies, or special diets, before commencing on any new area of the Taste Programme.
   — Discuss with parents, and send home, the section on 'taste' in the Sensory Questionnaire.
   — Have someone else record reactions, if possible, to enable an objective recording to be taken.
   — Use a video camera for in-depth, freeze-frame analysis of reactions.
   — Decide the objective of the lesson beforehand and *keep* to this lesson objective.
   — Check that all materials are ready and available.

2 *The child in the taste area*
   — Talk to the child beforehand and let him know what is going to happen *before* you do anything.
   — Take the child to the Taste Area, explaining where you are going and what will happen.
   — Check that the child is positioned comfortably and that *you* are also comfortable.
   — Keep to the lesson objective.
   — Prepare the taste sample(s) using clean utensils and/or clean fingers.
   — Tell the child what taste sample is to be given and be very encouraging in eliciting a response from him.
   — Allow the child to have a good smell of the taste sample prior to the actual tasting.
   — Leave strong tastes to the end of a taste session. Be very careful with fiery tastes. Do not cause discomfort.
   — Place the taste sample in a variety of positions in the mouth, eg. on the tongue, on the lips, near the lips, sides of the mouth and palate, etc.
   — Observe and record whilst watching.
   — Allow time for the taste to make an impact on the child.
   — Give the child a drink to clean the palate between taste samples.
   — Most importantly, remember to highlight tastes in any new situations where the taste may occur. Talk to the

child. Remind the child that the taste has occurred before, and now, 'here it is again!' in a new situation.
— Tell the child when the taste testing is finished and praise his co-operation or achievement.
— Tell the child what is going to happen next and move him to the appropriate area.

3   *After the tasting session*
   — Check recordings and plan the next step.
   — Repeat and repeat tastes, even if there is no reaction— there may be one soon.
   — Let the family know what progress is being made and occasionally send home some 'fun homework'.
   — Remember to include dinner ladies and other members of staff who deal with the child in the planning and execution of the Taste Programme. They may have different approaches and different ideas to contribute to the programme, increasing its value to the child and its ultimate success.

5   Taste Curriculum—Action Checklist
1   Read relevant books and articles.
2   See relevant films.
3   Visit other schools and review their Taste Banks and Curricula.
4   Begin collecting taste samples with which to equip your own Taste Bank.
5   Plan a Taste Curriculum with main aims, goals, and units.
6   Plan a recording system.
7   Involve parents and other people important to the child.
8   Plan and equip the Taste Bank.
9   Keep everything up to date (objectives, records, taste samples, etc.).
10   Keep adding new tastes to the Taste Bank.
11   Evaluate the Taste Curriculum and Taste Bank regularly.

6   Helpful Books and Articles
Please refer to the main bibliography in Chapter 1 for general information that will help in developing a sensory curriculum and also help with recording and assessment.

Anderson, C. (1983). *Feeding—A Guide to Assessment and Intervention with Handicapped Children.* Obtainable from: Publications Department, Jordanhill College of Education, Southbrae Drive, Glasgow G13 1PP.

Andrews, M. F. (1978). 'Taste the Sound of Raindrops', in *Journal of Creative Behaviour,* vol. 12, part 3, pp. 151–3.

Browning, M. M. (1983). *Identifying the Needs of Profoundly Mentally Handicapped Children.* Part 3 (on functioning of the senses). Obtainable from: Publications Department, Jordanhill College of Education, Southbrae Drive, Glasgow G13 1PP.

Carr, J. (1980). *Helping your Handicapped Child.* Part 2, Section 12, 'Eating and Tablemanners'. Harmondsworth: Penguin Books.

Cordle, M. *Feeding Can Be Fun.* Obtainable from: The Spastics Society, 12 Park Crescent, London W1N 4EQ.

Finnie, N. R. (1975). *Handling the Young Cerebral Palsied Child at Home.* Chapter 9, 'Feeding'. Sunrise Books, E P Dutton.

Freeman, P. (1975). *Understanding the Deaf/Blind Child.* Information on feeding, taste, and texture. London: Heinemann.

Freeman, P. (1971). *A Parent's Guide to the Early Care of a Deaf/Blind Child.* Sections on Feeding. Obtainable from: National Deaf/Blind and Rubella Association (SENSE), 311 Grays Inn Road, London WC1X 8PT.

Holle, B. (1976). *Motor Development in Children: Normal and Retarded.* Chapter on Taste and Smell. Oxford: Blackwell Scientific Publications.

Harkness, C., and Sandys, H. *Teaching a Handicapped Child to Feed.* Obtainable from: Friends of the Cheyne Centre for Spastic Children, 63 Cheyne Walk, London SW3 5LT.

Kitzinger, M. (1980). 'Planning the management of feeding in the visually handicapped child', in *Child: care, health and development*, vol. 6, pp 291–9.

Mitchell, A. (ed.) (1982).*Your Child Is Different.* Chapter 5, 'Feeding Is More than Eating and Drinking'. London: George Allen and Unwin.

Newson, E., and Hipgrave, T. (1982). *Getting through to Your Handicapped Child.* Chapter 6, Section on 'Feeding', and Chapter 7, Section on 'Helping a Child to Think about Tastes'. Cambridge University Press.

Ratcliff, J. D. 'I Am John's Tongue'. from *The Reader's Digest,* 1983, pp. 82-5.
Warner, J. (1981). *Helping the Handicapped Child with Early Feeding.* Obtainable from: PTM, 23 Horn Street, Winslow, Buckinghamshire MK18 3AP.

4 DEVELOPING A SMELL CURRICULUM AND SMELL BANK

Contents

1 Introduction

WHY A SMELL CURRICULUM?

By using the sense of smell, the very special child can discover more about the world around him. The sensory cells in the nose can be used to discriminate smells, gain new information, and also to evoke memories.

— The smell of tobacco may equal a liked person.
— The smell of fur may mean the family dog.
— The smell of lavender water may link to granny.

— The smell of grass may be associated with the garden and sunshine.
— The smell of dinner cooking may anticipate feeding.

THE LINK TO A CHILD'S TASTE AND FEEDING PROGRAMME
The development of a child's awareness and discrimination of smells is linked very closely to taste. The brain mingles together the two messages of smell and taste for better sensory interpretation.

The smell of food should help the child's progress in his Feeding Programme. The child may begin to anticipate food before tasting, and be more prepared for the food.

The recommendations from the chapter on Taste should be used in conjunction with those in this chapter when designing a curriculum with maximum impact for the child. These two chapters should not be used separately, especially in the area of feeding.

2   Planning a Smell Curriculum

SETTING YOUR AIMS
The main aim for the Smell Curriculum should be to enable the child to become aware of smells, to use this awareness of smells to learn from new experiences, and to help in the development of taste.

SETTING YOUR GOALS
The goals that are set for the Smell Curriculum are neither developmental nor taught in sequence. The sense of smell is acute in some people and non-existent in others. A person with a heavy cold can lose all sense of smell.

The very special child is no different, and will have personal preferences for smells, or perhaps little interest in smell. The goals set should not be set in isolation, and will link with other areas of the curriculum. For example, the goal of 'increased body movements' would link strongly to the child's Movement Programme and Multisensory Programme.

Below is a list of some possible main goals:
— stimulation and awareness of smells,
— increased awareness of smells linked to tastes,

— improved feeding,
— simple discrimination of smells,
— 'location' link to smells,*
— increased toleration to handling,
— increased head movement,
— increased body movement,
— beginning of inhalation using the nose,
— beginning of memory, remembering and recognising smells.

One or two goals would be taken for a particular child, to be used as priority areas in feeding.

PLANNING SMELL UNITS

There is a variety of main areas to use for the foundation of a Smell Curriculum. These areas could include smells that are:

pleasant   unpleasant   familiar   unfamiliar
human   domestic   locational

The Taste Bank will also provide a wide variety of tastes with associated smells. Some examples of smell units from the curriculum follow:

CURRICULUM DATA
Pleasant Smells

Curriculum area   : Cognitive
Main objective   : Sensory development
Stage   : Smells—pleasant
Resources   : School curriculum

---

1 Indifferent to pleasant smells.
2 Responds to pleasant smells.
3 Rejects pleasant smells.
4 Shows preference for pleasant smells.
5 Chooses pleasant smells from a range of smells presented.
6 Other.

---

* 'locational' smells could be:
  soap   = bathroom
  wood and straw = the rabbit hutch
  warm oily smell = school boiler room
  clay   = art room

CURRICULUM DATA

Unpleasant/Strong Smells

Curriculum area : Cognitive
Main objective : Sensory development
Stage : Smells—unpleasant/strong
Resources : School curriculum

1 Indifferent to unpleasant smells.
2 Responds to unpleasant smells.
3 Rejects unpleasant smells.
4 Shows preference for unpleasant smells.
5 Discriminates unpleasant smells from a range of smells presented.
6 Other.

CURRICULUM DATA

Familiar/Situational Smells

Curriculum area : Cognitive
Main objective : Sensory development
Stage : Smells—familiar/situational
Resources : School curriculum

1 Is indifferent to familiar smells.
2 Responds to familiar smells in familiar contexts.
3 Rejects familiar smells in familiar contexts.
4 Responds to familiar smells in unfamiliar contexts.
5 Rejects familiar smells in unfamiliar contexts.
6 Discriminates between familiar smells.
7 Shows preference for certain familiar smells.
8 Other.

CURRICULUM DATA

Domestic Smells

Curriculum area : Cognitive
Main objective : Sensory development
Stage : Smells—domestic
Resources : School curriculum

1   Is indifferent to domestic smells.
2   Responds to domestic smells.
3   Rejects domestic smells.
4   Shows situational awareness of domestic smells.
5   Discriminates between a range of domestic smells.
6   Other.

3   Linking the Child to the Smell Curriculum

THE FAMILY CAN HELP

The home, or other caring environment, provides a wide range of smell experiences for the child. There are certain smells that are unique to the child's home and which may evoke memory if smelt outside the home.

Observations from the home will provide some information on the child's sense of smell, but it is a sense that is not usually observed in detail. However, a simple Sensory Questionnaire (see Appendix C for sample Sensory Questionnaire) discussed with and completed by the family, should provide useful information.

A Parent Workshop in the sensory area of smell will help explain the aims of developing the child's sense of smell. This involvement of the family can lead to added awareness of the importance of smell, especially in the areas of taste and feeding.

'Fun' homework can be sent home (see Appendix B for a sample Homework Card). For example, the RNIB Odour Box (see p. 107) could be sent home for the weekend. Perhaps some home smells, such as a certain perfume, hairspray, or deodorant used by a special member of the family, could be sent to the school for testing sessions.

THE SCHOOL CAN HELP

Information can be collected at school to form the basis of the child's Smell Programme. A simple recording form can be used to collect the pertinent information (see Appendix C, Simple Recording Sheets). This record should be kept over a given period of time during which a range of smells should be given. There is a range of reactions, and non-reactions, to be observed and used as the first steps of an individual Smell Programme.

THE CHILD CAN HELP

The child provides valuable information which helps to form the basis of the Smell Programme. This information is gathered through careful observation of the child by staff. In this way, the programme can be child-directed, not adult orientated, and will be at the level appropriate to the individual child. In other words, each child should have a unique Smell Curriculum.

The following example shows some of the range of reactions which may be observed from a child during a smell recording. Remember, some children react in the most unexpected ways. The teacher's knowledge of the child will help in interpretation.

CURRICULUM DATA
Range of Reactions

Curriculum area   :   Cognitive
Main objective   :   Sensory development
Stage   :   Reactions to smells
Resources   :   School curriculum

RANGE OF REACTIONS

1   Facial Expressions
   1.1   Eyes widen.
   1.2   Nostrils dilate.
   1.3   Screws up nose.
   1.4   Smiles.
   1.5   Frowns.
   1.6   Blinks rapidly.

2   Movement Changes
   2.1   Stills.
   2.2   Startles.
   2.3   Stops hand mannerisms.
   2.4   Increases hand mannerisms.
   2.5   Shudders.
   2.6   Turns head away.
   2.7   Moves nearer to smell.
   2.8   Sniffs smell.
   2.9   Tracks smell by turning head.
   2.10 Rubs nose with arm.

3 Mouth and Tongue Movements
   3.1 Salivates.
   3.2 Sucking movements.
   3.3 Lips close tightly.
   3.4 Spits.
4 Noise Expressions
   4.1 Moans.
   4.2 Cries.
   4.3 Coos.
   4.4 Laughs.
   4.5 Shouts.
5 Smell Connections
   5.1 Connects smell with disliked taste or situation.
   5.2 Connects smell with liked taste or situation.

6 Other

To demonstrate how this information is collected, the recording opposite shows some of the child's reactions to a variety of smells over a period of one month. From an analysis of the recordings over the entire period came the main objectives: 'to increase response to toilet-linked smells and routines' and 'to increase locational awareness of the toileting area'. These objectives were closely linked to the area of self-help skills.

OTHER PROFESSIONALS CAN HELP
Other professionals can help in planning a smell programme. A multidisciplinary approach will enlist the help and support of the speech therapist, physiotherapist, occupational therapist, dietician, and others. They will help with comfortable positioning, equipment, and smell suggestions.

The aromatherapist is another professional who can be enlisted to help in the programme. Aromatherapy is the practice of using strong aromatic oils to massage into the body for ailments, and also general well-being. Aromatherapists can be located at Health Farms or Therapeutic Centres.

Further information is obtainable from: the College of Natural Therapies and Aesthetic Treatments, 22 Bromley Road, London SE6.

RECORDING FORM

Sensory Area: Smell   Name: Brenda

Materials	Date	Exposure	Response	Comments
1) toilet freshener	Tues	To nose. Intermittent.	Grimaced. Turned away.	Bathroom area and 'smells' corner.
2) soap— highly perfumed	Thur	Washed hands —five minutes.	No apparent reaction, hands floppy, body floppy.	Bathroom area —supported on my lap.
3) talc	Fri	On hands and bottom. —five minutes during changing	No apparent reaction, lay very still.	Bathroom area —on changing platform.
4) Disinfectant	Tues	Smelling strip. Intermittent.	Blinked, grimaced on both occasions.	Bathroom area— smells corner on floor.

4   The Smell Bank

WHAT IS A SMELL BANK?

A Smell Bank is part of a Sensory Bank. It is a resource to complement the Smell Curriculum. It is used to stimulate a wide range of experiences in smell. It is closely linked to the Taste Bank, and many of the materials in these two 'stores' are the same or interchangeable, especially in the area of feeding.

Part of a Smell Bank includes smells that cannot be stored in bottles. They are the smells linked to the environment, a person, or an experience. These are an essential part of the smell experience for the child and should form an integral part of the Smell Bank. These smells would be recorded on a special card and used for each individual child.

BEGINNING A SMELL BANK

An area of the classroom should be named as the learning area for smell. There is also a variety of locations that could be designated as smell areas, especially those important to the experience of the child. These may include areas such as the kitchen, the pottery room, the inside of a car, or the local café or park.

The smells should be stored in an easily accessible trolley or cupboard with reasonably sized trays or boxes for the separate

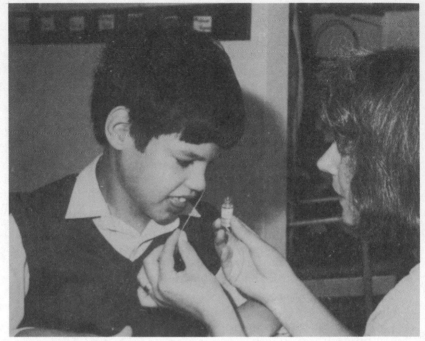

Ian concentrates on smelling honeysuckle from a smelling strip.

smell units. Dangerous materials, such as domestic smells, should always be located in the teacher's cupboard, on a high shelf, and suitably marked as dangerous. All smells that may be dangerous to anyone should be highly diluted from the original substance. One safe way to present them would be on cotton-wool moistened with the diluted liquid. The moist cotton-wool is kept in a capped container. Even if the children in the room are immobile, there are always the curious children who come to use the room during the day.

The smells should be kept in capped bottles or tubes and a supply of smelling strips or cotton buds kept readily available. The condition and strength of the smells should be regularly checked for deterioration. New smells should be added to the Smell Bank as they become available or relevant to a specific child's needs. The smells should be divided into separate sections to suit *your* Smell Curriculum.

SUGGESTIONS FOR SECTIONS IN A SMELL BANK

It is important to make sure that each smell section is clearly labelled, and that each smell is labelled, to allow easy and accurate access to the smells. No smells should be used that you would not use yourself, eg. petrol, glue, ammonia, bleach.

The following smell sections are useful as examples:

perfumed	household	cleaning
medicinal	aromatic	herbal
spiced	sneezy	leather and cloth
toilet	bathroom	male/female
odour box (RNIB)		

Many of the smells will be found in the Taste Bank and should be duplicated in the Smell Bank, if necessary. It is preferable, however, to use the smells and tastes together. For example, the smell of an orange being peeled would link to the taste as the orange was eaten or tasted by the child.

Here are some smells that could be used in some of the mentioned smell units. Warning! Please ensure that all materials used for smelling are NON-TOXIC. Some smells may need diluting.

Household
(used in conjunction
with the relevant activity)
shoe cleaning materials
furniture cleaning
   materials
dishwashing materials
kitchen cleaning materials
—these would be stored
   in separate boxes,
   i.e. shoe cleaning =
variety of polishes
polishing cloth
brush
and actually *used* with
the child to link smell
with experience

Perfumed
hairsprays
wide variety of perfumes
bath cubes
deodorants
scented pieces of cloth
shampoos
bubble bath
soaps
   —these would also be in
   general use in smell
   areas such as the
   bathroom

Herbal
a range of growing herbs
dried herbs
herbal syrups
dried flowers
dried leaves
a range of *pot-pourris*
herbal pillows
herbal bags (in a mobile)
(Seek the assistance of a
herbalist)

Smells to tickle the nose
(minute amounts to be used)
snuff
pepper
balsam
Vick
certain spices

Herbal and spice perfumes
(from Body Shop)
herb sleep pillow
herb snore pillow
Fandangles—aromas on
ropes
amphora pots—clay pots
to allow perfume oil to
scent a room
essential balm
linen drawer sachets—
sandalwood
a range of perfume oils
Elizabethan wash balls
herbs and *pot-pourri*
smells/aroma
disc player from: Toys
for the Handicapped
(see p. 37).

Smells to add to water
(from Body Shop)
rose/musk/herb bath oils
strawberry body shampoo
orange cream bath oil
raspberry ripple bath oil
and bathing bubbles
bath oil beads
bath salts
superior bath oil powder
herbal bath tablets
tea rose/samarkand talcs

USING THE SMELL BANK AND CURRICULUM WITH A CHILD

1 *Preparations beforehand*
— Refer to the child's records for any medical condition,
allergies, or special factors *before* commencing on any
new areas of the Smell Programme.
— Send home, and discuss, the section on smell in the
Sensory Questionnaire.

- Have someone else record reactions, if possible, to enable an objective recording to be taken.
- Use a video camera, for in-depth freeze-frame analysis.
- Check that all materials are ready and available.
- Decide the lesson objective beforehand, and keep to that objective

2 *The child in the smell area*
  - Take the child to the smell area (or smell area outside the room), explaining where you are going and what will happen.
  - Talk to the child beforehand, explaining what is going to happen *before* you do anything.
  - Check that the child is comfortable—and that you yourself are comfortable.
  - Check that all recording materials or video camera are at hand. Do not record every session, perhaps one out of five, but record any significant points in between.
  - Make sure that the objective of the recording session is followed.
  - Tell the child which smell objects he will be smelling, and be very encouraging to him.
  - Allow the child to have a good smell.
  - Link the smell to the taste object if appropriate.
  - Allow time for the smell to have full impact.
  - Place the smell in a variety of positions, eg. near, far, above, close to, next to the nose.
  - Allow the child the opportunity to track a smell up, down, across the face, around the head, etc.
  - Encourage movement towards a smell.
  - Observe and record reactions—both facial and body movements.
  - Allow the smell to disappear before giving the next smell. Use the strongest smell at the end of the session or it will blot out weaker smells.
  - Tell the child when the smell session has finished and praise his participation.
  - Tell the child what is going to happen next and move him to the appropriate area.

3 *After the recording session*
— Check the recordings and plan the next steps as appropriate.
— Repeat smells again and again, even if there is no reaction—there may be a reaction one day.
— Let the family know what work the child has been doing with smells and send home some 'fun' homework occasionally.
— Do remember to include the other members of staff in the Smell Programme, i.e. those who work with the child during the day. Their smell may be a good source of learning for the child!
— Most important of all, remember to generalise the work done in smells with the child, especially in the areas of situation and location for the child.

5 Smell Curriculum—Action Checklist
1 Read relevant books and articles, and see relevant films.
2 Visit other schools and review their Smell Banks and Smell Curricula.
3 Begin collecting samples of smells with which to equip your Smell Bank.
4 Plan a Smell Curriculum, with main goals and units.
5 Plan a recording system.
6 Involve parents and other people who are important to the child.
7 Plan and equip a Smell Bank.
8 Keep everything up to date and keep adding new smells to the Smell Bank.
9 Evaluate the Smell Curriculum and Smell Bank regularly.

6 Helpful Books and Articles
Please refer to the main bibliography in Chapter 1 for general information that will help in developing a Sensory Curriculum and also help with recording and assessment.

NOTE: The booklist in the chapter on Taste is also relevant in the area of Smell.

Browning, M. M. (1983). *Identifying the Needs of Profoundly Mentally Handicapped Children*. Part 3 on Functioning of the Senses. Obtainable from: Publications Department, Jordanhill College of Education, Southbrae Drive, Glasgow G13 1PP.

Freeman, P. (1975). *Understanding the Deaf/Blind Child.* Section on Smell. London: Heinemann Medical Books.

Hinds, R. (1981). 'The Role of the Sense of Smell in the Lives of Young Children', in *Apex* magazine, 1981, pp 120-3.

Holle, B. (1976). *Motor Development in Children: Normal and Retarded.* Section on smell and taste. Oxford: Blackwell Scientific Publications.

Kybal, J. (1980). *Herbs and Spices.* London: Hamlyn.

Moncrieff, W. R. (1970). *Odours.* London: Heinemann.

Newson, E., and Hipgrave, T. (1982). *Getting through to Your Handicapped Child.* Chapter 7—section on Smell. Cambridge University Press.

Price, S. (1983). *Practical Aromatherapy—How to use essential oils to restore vitality.* Thorsons.

Shoesmith, K. (1973). *Scent and Smell.* Burke Books Limited.

Tisserand, R. (1985). *The Art of Aromatherapy.* C. W. Daniel Co. Limited.

The RNIB Odour Box. Obtainable, free, from: The Royal National Institute for the Blind, 224 Great Portland Street, London W1N 6AA. The Odour Box contains a range of unusual smells, such as grass and sweat. They should only be used with smelling strips or cotton buds.

5 DEVELOPING A SOUND CURRICULUM AND SOUND BANK

Contents

1 Introduction

WHY A SOUND CURRICULUM?

Very special children cannot make much sense of verbal communication. They also find it difficult to form speech and even basic sounds, as these are a most complex process to learn. However, an awareness of sounds can give them some understanding of the environment, as well as enjoyment of the beauty of certain sounds.

It is therefore important that special needs children achieve a certain level of understanding of sounds, especially those which are important to them. This will give them a greater awareness of both themselves and their environment. Whether or not speech is achieved, a child may learn to enjoy and derive pleasure from sounds as a simple leisure-time occupation.

THE LINK TO A CHILD'S COMMUNICATION PROGRAMME

Even if special children cannot use conventional means of communicating, such as speech or signing, they can still learn to make sense of the sounds around them. They can begin to communicate their needs through simple sounds, forming a highly individual communication programme. Even if initially only able to cry, sneeze, or yawn, they are beginning to learn the movements required to make sound.

The Sound Curriculum should be an integral part of the child's communication programme. A major prerequisite of language learning is the development of attention and listening skills. The role of these two skills should be emphasised in the link between the Sound Curriculum and the communication curriculum.

THE LINK TO A CHILD'S FEEDING PROGRAMME

The same parts of the mouth and throat are used for both feeding and making sounds. If the child feeds well, there is the possibility that meaningful sound may begin to appear. The range of movements in making sounds, ie. swallowing, sucking, biting, chewing, jaw movements, and opening and closing the lips, can all help towards improving a child's feeding programme.

THE LINK TO A CHILD'S MULTISENSORY PROGRAMME

The Multisensory Programme will incorporate many sounds, both human and musical, in each session. During these sessions, the child receives a bombardment of sounds, accompanying movement of the body and interaction with the immediate environment.

The development of a Sound Programme for the child can

enhance and expand this experience. The child may begin to make sense of sound and respond more readily through this multisensory approach. (See Chapter 8.)

2   Planning a Sound Curriculum

SETTING YOUR AIMS

The main aim of the Sound Curriculum should be to develop to the fullest the child's awareness and understanding of sound. This may lead to the opportunity for developing some form of communication based on sound, linked to any other means of communication for the child.

SETTING YOUR GOALS

Goals set for the Sound Curriculum are not set in graduated steps. There is not a developmental (incremental) set of goals in an area that is different for each individual. For example, some people enjoy classical music, others enjoy punk music, and still others enjoy country music. The same differences will apply to the special child, who will have a preference for certain sounds which will be enjoyed more than others.

The goals which are set should be interlinked to other areas of the curriculum. For example, the goal of 'use of sounds for tracking' may link strongly with a child's Cognitive Programme, Visual Tracking Programme, and Movement Programme, as well as helping with the Attention Programme.

The main goals may include some of the following:
— enjoyment of sounds,
— stimulation and awareness of sounds,
— increased tolerance of a range of sounds,
— improved listening skills,
— simple discrimination of sounds,
— increased tolerance of handling,
— increased movement of the body,
— increased movement of the head,
— beginning of vocalisation,
— beginning of communication,
— use of sounds to track,
— use of sounds to locate.

One or two of these goals would be selected and used for a particular child's Sound Programme.

PLANNING SOUND UNITS

A Sound Programme should include the sound areas of attention, localisation, discrimination, tracking, and general noise.

These main areas can be broken down into more precise units. For example, the discrimination of sound could include units for pitch, loud, soft, rhythms, time duration, and beat.

Examples of five curriculum units, including attention, discrimination, localisation, tracking and general noise, are illustrated in this section.

CURRICULUM DATA
Attention to Sound

Curriculum area : Cognitive
Main objective : Sensory development
Stage : Sound—attention
Resources : School curriculum, music adviser, teacher for the hearing impaired, and speech therapist

---

1   Is indifferent to any sounds presented.
2   Some attention given to familiar sounds.
3   Some attention given to unfamiliar sounds.
4   Some attention given to a range of sounds.
5   Measurable attention given to a range of sounds.
6   Other.

CURRICULUM DATA
Sound Discrimination

Curriculum area : Cognitive
Main objective : Sensory development
Stage : Sound—discrimination
Resources : School curriculum, music adviser, teacher for the hearing impaired, and speech therapist.

---

1   Is indifferent to:
   a)   range of pitch
   b)   range of loudness

      c) range of rhythm
      d) range of duration.
2 Discriminates between:
      a) range of pitches
      b) range of loudness
      c) range of rhythms
      d) range of duration of sounds.
3 Other.

CURRICULUM DATA
Localisation of Sound

Curriculum area : Cognitive
Main objective   : Sensory development
Stage   : Sound—localisation
Resources   : School curriculum, music adviser, teacher for the hearing impaired, and speech therapist.

---

1 Is indifferent to location of any sounds.
2 Shows some reaction to local familiar sounds.
3 Shows some location of familiar voice in a familiar environment.
4 Locates familiar sounds in unfamiliar environment.
5 Locates familiar voices in unfamiliar environment.
6 Reacts to specific sounds in the environment for location of position.
7 Reacts to sounds presented in a variety of positions and locations.
8 Other.

CURRICULUM DATA
Sound Tracking

Curriculum area : Cognitive
Main objective   : Sensory development
Stage   : Sound—tracking
Resources   : School curriculum, music adviser, teacher for the hearing impaired, and speech therapist.

1   Is indifferent to moving sounds.
2   Reacts to moving sounds with added clues, eg. brightly coloured blower.
3   Begins to track loud noises nearby.
4   Begins to track loud noises above the body.
5   Begins to track loud noises behind the body.
6   Begins to track loud noises in circular movements.
7   Follows sound with eyes.
8   Follows sound with whole head.
9   Follows sound with body.
10   Other.

CURRICULUM DATA
General Noises

Curriculum area   :   Cognitive
Main objective   :   Sensory development
Stage   :   Sound—general noises
Resources   :   School curriculum, music adviser, teacher for the hearing impaired, speech therapist.

---

1   Is indifferent to any range of sounds presented in a stimuli-free environment.
2   Reacts to range of sounds.
3   Reacts to local familiar or routine sounds.
4   Reacts to a familiar voice.
5   Reacts to a range of sounds after several presentations.
6   Reacts to a range of sounds after many presentations.
7   Other.

---

3   Linking the Child to the Sound Curriculum

THE FAMILY CAN HELP
The very special child has many experiences of sound at home or in other caring environments. Many of these sounds, which are familiar to the child, may prompt responses at school.

Information can be gained from home which will help in planning an individual Sound Programme. A simple sensory questionnaire, completed by the family, will give more information on sound and its importance to the child. (See Appendix A for sample Sensory Questionnaire). When compiling the Sound Programme, this information can then be discussed with the family.

A parent workshop in the area of sound will give the family a further opportunity to learn about the importance of sounds for the child. It will be an opportunity to discuss the aims and also the methods of increasing the child's awareness of sound. The family can also help by making home tapes of all the special sounds that evoke responses or pleasure from their child.

For example, a tape may contain:
— songs from a sister or brother,
— greetings from dad,
— the dog barking,
— granny knitting and chattering,
— a favourite tune,
— some favourite music,
— mum singing a lullaby, etc.

The family, especially siblings, can also help with 'fun' homework. (See Appendix B for a sample Homework Card). Homework might be a weekend of water noises or perhaps playing with a box of noisy mechanical toys sent home from school. A tape of the multisensory sessions enjoyed by the child at school may also be exciting homework for the child.

THE SCHOOL CAN HELP

Information about a child and his awareness of sounds can be collected at school using a simple recording system (See Appendix C for Simple Recording Sheets). Records should be kept over a period of time during which a range of reactions can be collected for planning the Sound Programme. There is a range of reactions, and non-reactions, to be used as the basis for the child's individual Sound Programme.

The following example shows the range of reactions which may be observed in a sound session at school.

CURRICULUM DATA
Range of Reactions

Curriculum area	:	Cognitive
Main objective	:	Sensory development
Stage	:	Range of reactions
Resources	:	School curriculum

RANGE OF REACTIONS
1 Startles.
2 Stills.
3 Facial expression changes.
   a) Blinks rapidly.
   b) Smiles.
   c) Frowns.
4 Turns head to source of sound.
5 Follows sound by moving head.
6 Strong increase in movement.
   a) Bounces.
   b) Kicks.
   c) Waves arms and/or legs.
   d) Moves trunk.
7 Follows sound by movement towards source.
8 Vocalises.
   a) Laughs.
   b) Shouts.
   c) Coos.

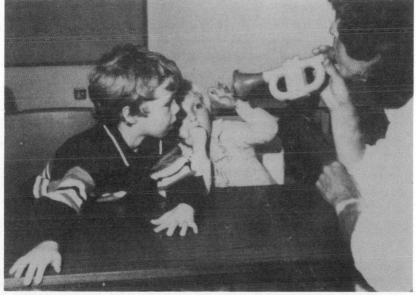

Tom and Amy react to a loud sound from the trumpet in different physical ways.

d) Shrieks.
e) Gurgles.
f) Blows bubbles.
g) Grinds teeth.
h) Cries or sobs.
9 Makes sound for self.
a) Knocking a hanging instrument.
b) Hitting a hanging instrument.
c) Grasping a hanging instrument.
10 Other.

THE CHILD CAN HELP

The child 'helps' by giving information through responses to sound. This information can be observed and recorded using a simple recording system. To show how the information is collected, the following data show several of the recordings of a child's reaction to sounds over a period of time.

From all the recordings taken came the main objective for the child, ie. 'to build up a tolerance of loud noises'. This linked closely with objectives set in the Self-Help area, ie. 'to tolerate being in assembly without crying'.

RECORDING FORM

Sensory Area: Sound   Name: Sally

Materials	Date	Exposure	Response	Comments
1) cymbals —soft —loud		over 3 minutes, interval between.	Startled and cried at loud cymbal. —very disturbed.	Lying on side on floor. —comforted when cried. —did not repeat loud cymbal.
2) newspapers —crinkled —torn into strips		5 minutes.	Blinked at torn paper sound and moved head slightly away —moved hands in torn strips, with physical prompt, to make noise.	On floor supported by my lap —paper all around the child.
3) Extending squeaker (feathered end).		2 minutes.	—Startled. —Turned away. —Frowned. —Brought arm up to push squeaker away.	Lying on side on floor.

OTHER PROFESSIONALS CAN HELP

Information and help from other professionals is needed in planning individual Sound Programmes. The multidisciplinary approach is of great benefit in planning these programmes. The physiotherapist and occupational therapist can help with comfortable positioning and adapted equipment. The speech therapist can help with linking the sounds to a Communication Programme.

The teacher for the deaf can also help with planning these programmes. She has particular expertise in this area, which is relevant to the hearing child as well as to the hearing-impaired child. Such teachers can monitor programmes over the year, provide extended programmes, and help with acoustic or hearing aids.

The medical team, including the paediatrician, can help with regular checks on each child's hearing. These regular hearing evaluations, even for the profoundly deaf child, will monitor any changes, such as temporary deafness or the need for new aids.

It is helpful for a teacher as well as the parents, to accompany a child to a hearing evaluation session. Even better would be for the hearing specialist to come to the school for the evaluation, and to meet the parents and staff together, ie. to help instil the team approach.

The music adviser in the county can also provide expertise and resources to help in planning Sound Programmes, especially in the musical area.

4   The Sound Bank

WHAT IS A SOUND BANK?

The Sound Bank complements the Sound Curriculum. It provides resources for use in stimulating a wide range of sound experiences. Development of the Sound Bank is also an instrumental part in establishing the school's Communication Curriculum.

BEGINNING A SOUND BANK

An area of the room should be designated for sound. By its nature, this area requires careful positioning in order to avoid disrupting other areas of the room. For example, it is not a good idea to have a noisy sound area next to a quiet, peaceful area. It would be more appropriate next to an active area. This does not preclude sounds being quiet and peaceful.

The music room should be seen as an extension of the sound area in the classroom, and should provide a wide range of sound experiences. If possible, for the special child who is ultra-sensitive to sounds, it is desirable to have a sound area in a stimuli-free room, progressing the child to the normal environment by stages.

Materials should be stored in a convenient storage unit or cupboard with reasonably-sized boxes or containers. Each storage container should be clearly labelled with the materials it contains and the range of sounds these materials can produce. These materials should be regularly checked for replacement and additions to create new sounds in the stipulated range. The materials should be kept away from children when not in use, to prevent disruption either of the materials themselves or of their proper storage.

The sound area may also have certain sound-producing/recording equipment available for general use. For example:
— small electric organ,
— recorder/radio cassette,
— walkman radios with very light earphones,
— large box to use as acoustic box with music materials.

SUGGESTIONS FOR SECTIONS IN A SOUND BANK
Each section in the Sound Bank should be clearly labelled to permit easy access for the particular sounds required during a session. Typical sound sections should include:

loud	soft	harsh	vibratory	percussion
whistles	wood	brass	squeakers	tick-tock
drums	bells	noises—paper, mechanical, blowing		

Some sounds will be repeated in different sections. For example, a drum could be in the loud, vibratory, and percussion areas, as well as 'drums'. The Table shows how some of the sounds could be used in the suggested sections.

TABLE—TYPICAL SOUNDS FOR SOUND BANK SECTIONS

Tick-tock noises
alarm clocks
Fisher-Price clock
watch with loud tick
one bead in a container
metronome

Blowing noises
range of squeakers
toy trumpets
whoopee cushion
bubbler and bubble pipe
empty plastic bottle
empty spray bottle
hollow pipes
balloons
straws

Drums
tambour
tambourine
snare drum
bass drum
timpani
finger tomtom
hand drum
rubber drum
steel drum
empty containers
tabor drum
Gato drum

Whistles
siren
acme thunderer
steamboat whistle
bird warbles
   (available from Brady Brothers
   Ltd.)

Paper noises
cellophanes
greaseproof paper
chocolate box wrappings
paper to tear
tissue paper
newspaper
paperback to flick
large sheets of crinkly, shiny paper
   (to wrap around child)

Tapes
home tapes
school tapes
outside noises
children's own noises
staff voices
special school concerts and
   assemblies
multisensory tapes
range of commercial music tapes
   from Communication
   Curriculum
routine sound tapes, eg. 'Look
   Hear!' tape from LDA (see
   Suppliers. Covers human, daily,
   home, school, transport and
   animal noises).
music—folk
      jazz
      rock
      Indian
      Maori
      Japanese
      Chinese
      church organ
      choirs
      taped live music
      (Let the children make a
      tape of 'their' music, and
      use an environmental
      control system switch to
      allow them to choose to
      turn tape recorder on to
      listen.)

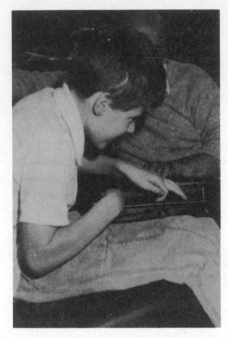

Simon makes sounds on the zither and concentrates on the vibration of the wires.

Sample Music Linked to Sound Programme

Here are some suggestions for a Music/Sound Programme Lesson of 30 minutes' duration. There are five components for the lesson:

1   *Name rhythms*, using Christian names and perhaps surnames. Experiment with pitched and unpitched instruments, eg.

    John-ee   2 chime bars
    Su-zann-ah   3 drum beats
    Flo-rence   2 maraca shakes

    This will provide a 'signature tune' for each child.
    Two or three names can be strung together to make a tune.
    Use the same 'signature' tune for each session.

2   *Sounds to accompany simple songs/poems*
    Examples—for young children

    Hickory Dickory Dock (claves—tick-tock)
    Mouse ran up clock   (ascending swanee whistle)
    Clock struck one   (gong, cymbal)

       Mouse ran down   (descending swanee whistle)
       Hickory Dickory Dock (claves)
       Jingle Bells (bells)
The children should be involved in making the sounds, so that they become part of the production.

Use songs with a very quiet or no accompaniment, or simple poems with a strong rhythm and obvious rhyme.

Repeat the same songs to encourage anticipation, and introduce new ones to increase range.

Use age appropriate songs for all participants.

3 *Sounds to attract attention*
Suggestions:

Metronome with tinsel/shiny paper attached to moving parts.

Stringed instruments—so that vibrations can be felt.

Guitars—children's hands to strum strings, back of guitar pressed against child's head.

Unusual sounds—factory hooters, lorry air horns, etc.

Clarinet—full range—can produce very high and very low sounds, plus tie dangly things to the instrument when being used.

Piano—have children sitting very close to it and/or touching it while it is being played to reinforce sound with vibration.

Whistles, party blowers, burst balloons for very loud/sharp noises.

4 *Songs and sounds to create moods*
Keep instruments in one category, eg.

Fear	*Calm*	*Happy*	*Noisy*
Drum	Chime Bar	Xylophone	Tambourine
Cymbal	Glockenspiel	Maracas	Castanets
Piano	Guitar	Swanee Whistle	Claves

Differentiate between instruments played loudly and loud instruments.

Use vocal sounds to augment instruments.

Darken/lighten room to add effect, eg. all get under a parachute and listen in the dark.

Use standard classical pieces to improve or complement, eg. *The Planets Suite:* 'Mars'—Fear.

5   *Listening to music*
Spend the last five minutes relaxing and listening to music
before saying 'goodbye'.

There are many styles of music, and some are easily
forgotten. Music which we cannot make sense of or dismiss
as frivolous, noisy, or 'not music', may well appeal to
children; here are some examples:
   Jazz—traditional and contemporary.
   'Modern'—Stockhausen.
   Electronic—Oldfield, Wakeman, Hansson.
   Early music.
   Heavy Metal.
   Folk—The Chieftains, Dubliners.
   Rock.
   Baroque.
   Instrumental—'The Flight of the Bumble Bee', 'Tubby
      the Tuba'.
   Choral—Kodaly, Handel, Britten.
   Also: the vast range of the usual classical and pop
      records.
   BBC Sound Effects records.
   Stereo testing records.

USING THE SOUND BANK AND CURRICULUM WITH A CHILD

1   *Preparations beforehand*
   —   Refer to the child's records for hearing tests and reports.
       This information will mean that the child will be placed
       in the best position to hear sounds. For example, a child
       with poor hearing in the left ear should have sounds
       presented to the right ear, or a child with a profound
       hearing handicap would require vibratory sounds.
   —   Send home and discuss the section on sound in the
       Sensory Questionnaire.
   —   Have someone else record reactions, if possible, to
       enable an objective recording to be taken.
   —   Use a video, if possible, to help with objective recording
       and to permit freeze-frame analysis later.
   —   Decide the objective of the lesson beforehand and keep
       to this objective.
   —   Check that materials are ready and available.

2   *The child in the sound area*
—   Make sure any hearing device or aid is functioning correctly for the child.
—   Talk to the child beforehand and let him know what is going to happen *before* you do anything.
—   Take the child to the sound area, explaining where you are going, and again telling the child what will happen.
—   Check that the positioning of the child is best for his hearing and also comfortable.
—   Ensure that you are comfortable.
—   Check that recording materials are at hand. Do not record every session, perhaps one out of five, but record any significant points in between.
—   Keep to the lesson objective.
—   Produce the sounds one at a time.
—   Take time with each sound.
—   Repeat the sounds as often as necessary.
—   If the child reacts, then reinforce the reaction: eg. 'What's that? Did you hear that?' and touch ears, etc.
—   Link the sound to another sense if necessary, eg. noisy ticking clock, crinkly shiny paper, etc.
—   Investigate the source of the sound together.
—   Encourage the child to respond.
—   Tell the child when the session has finished and praise his work.
—   Tell the child what is going to happen next and move to the appropriate area.

3   *After the sound session*
—   Check recordings and plan next step as appropriate.
—   Repeat and repeat sounds, even if there is no reaction. There may be a reaction one day.
—   Include other people in the child's Sound Programme, as they may approach the sound area in a different way, which may well succeed.
—   Let the family know what work the child has been doing with sounds and send home some 'fun' homework from time to time.
—   Most important of all, generalise sounds into other situations, for example:

Linking sound to a routine		*Locational sound*	
tapping spoon	= dinner	bead curtain	= door
car hooter	= taxi is here	spin dryer	= near splash pool
running tap	= wash time	tinkling bells	= mobile area
musical bell	= music time	typewriter	= secretary

5 Sound Curriculum—Action Checklist

1 Read relevant books and articles, and view films.
2 Visit other schools and see their Sound Banks and Curricula in action.
3 Consult with music professionals.
4 Begin collecting materials to equip your own Sound Bank.
5 Plan a Sound Curriculum with main aims, goals, and units.
6 Plan a recording system.
7 Involve parents and other people important to the child.
8 Plan, organise, and equip your Sound Bank.
9 Keep Sound Bank materials up to date and renew broken sound-producing materials.
10 Evaluate the Sound Curriculum and Sound Bank regularly.

6 Helpful Equipment

EQUIPMENT	SUGGESTED SUPPLIER
A good, strong record player, of the type which can be sat on for vibrations.	Coomber Limited, Croftwalk, near Pitchcroft, Worcs. WR1 3NZ
Musical instruments and shakers, tied near a child's reach and in view. Musical mobiles suspended very near to the child.	
Resonance Board—covered in a range of objects and materials for child's free use: this is a hollow platform to make sounds vibrate and resonate through the child via touch.	More information is available from: Lilli Nielson, child Welfare Consultant, Refsnoesskolen, Kystvenjen, DK 4400 Kalundborg, Denmark.

Sound bubble—noises and lights connected to pressure pads.	T F H, 76 Barracks Road, Sandy Lane Industrial Estate, Stourport on Severn, Worcs. DY13 9EX.
Sound tapes ('Look Hear').	LDA, Duke Street, Wisbech, Cambs PE13 2AE.
Range of durable, noisy toys, such as Singing Frogs or the Farmer Says, etc.	Toys from Mattel and Fisher Price available from toy shops.
Noise makers (sirens, bird warblers, etc.)	Brady Brothers Limited, Halesowen, West Midlands, B63 3AH.
Wide range of musical instruments from various countries.	Acorn Percussion, Unit 34, Abbey Business Centre, Ingate Place, London SW8 3NS.
Soundbeam equipment which enables anyone to make music and sounds by the slightest movements.	EMS Soundbeam, 87 Mill Hill Road, Norwich NR2 3DR.
A wide supply of musical instruments, recorded music and books from around the world	Knock on Wood, Arch X, Granary Wharf, Canal Basin, Leeds LS1 4BR.
A wide range of musical instruments.	London Music Shop, Bedwas House Industrial Estate, Bedwas, Newport, Gwent NP1 8XQ.
Audiotapes of music for relaxation and multisensory rooms.	New Experience, 27 Market Place, Penzance, Cornwall TR18 2JD. *also* New World Cassettes, Paradise Farm, Westhall, Halesworth, Suffolk IP19 8RH.

7   Helpful Books, Articles and Societies

Please refer to the main bibliography in Chapter 1 for general information that will help in developing a Sensory Curriculum and also help with recording and assessment.

Bower, T. (1977). *The Perceptual World of the Child.* Section on Sound. London: Open Books.

Dale, F. J. (1977). 'Progress Guide for "Deaf/Blind" and/or Severely Handicapped Children'. Obtainable from: National Deaf-Blind and Rubella Association (SENSE), 311 Grays Inn Road, London WC1X 8PT.

Freeman, P. (1971). *A Parent's Guide to the Early Care of a Deaf/Blind Child—Part 1.* Obtainable from: SENSE (address as above).

Freeman, P. (1975). *Understanding the Deaf/Blind Child.* London: Heinemann Medical Books.

Holle, B. (1976). *Motor Development in Children: Normal and Retarded.* Part II—section on hearing. Oxford: Blackwell Scientific Publications.

Kiernan, C., and Jones, M. C. (1982). *Behaviour Assessment Battery.* Part 5—Auditory (test and interview). Windsor: NFER/Nelson

Kiernan, C., Reid, B., and Goldbart, J. (1987). *Foundations of Communication and Language.* Staff training package for people working with very special people. Manchester University Press.

Newson, E., and Hipgrave, T. (1982). *Getting through to your Handicapped Child.* Chapter 7—section on 'Helping a child to listen'. Cambridge University Press

Nolan, M., and Tucker, I. G. (1988). *The Hearing Impaired Child and the Family*, 2nd ed. London: Souvenir Press.

Wood, M. (1982). *Music for Living.* Published by British Institute of Mental Handicap, Wolverhampton Road, Kidderminster, Worcs.

The Nadbrhc Schedule of Communication Development in Deaf/Blind Children (1979). Obtainable from: SENSE (address as above).

HELPFUL SOCIETIES

The following societies have a range of publications, leaflets, etc., available and are very willing to help with any problems you may encounter.

SENSE, 11-13 Clifton Terrace, Finsbury Park, London N4 3SR.

Royal National Institute for the Deaf, 105 Gower Street, London WC1E 6AH.

6 DEVELOPING A TACTILE CURRICULUM AND TACTILE BANK

Contents

1 Introduction

WHY A TACTILE CURRICULUM?

The very special child is constantly being touched, turned, handled, and placed in a variety of positions. The child is handled for feeding, cleaning, changing, etc., unable to escape from the touch of other people. Such children cannot understand some of the touches, nor complain or praise the quality of the touch. Their physical limitations prevent them from moving to and exploring tactile situations.

Thus, the child has to be helped to understand touch and other tactile experiences, in order to gain information and knowledge of experiences which we take for granted. The Tactile Curriculum and Tactile Bank should help the child gain a wider range of tactile experiences which will help him to begin to understand touch.

This curriculum involves the whole body, not just the hands and mouth. The most important resource in the Tactile Bank is the *human being* who is working with the child. The child must be able to touch people, even if this means having his arms or hands manipulated in order to touch and show affection or dislike.

THE LINK TO A CHILD'S MULTISENSORY PROGRAMME
The multisensory experience relies heavily on touch and tactile experience for the child. There is a very close physical touching bond between the child and his partner. The partner works closely with the child to try to encourage a two-way relationship, with touch as a very strong component. (The section on the Multisensory Programme presents much more information on this approach.)

THE LINK TO A CHILD'S BODY AWARENESS PROGRAMME
The Tactile Curriculum links closely to the development of a child's body awareness. The stimulation of tactile awareness will help him become more aware of the extent of his body as he is involved in the Tactile Programme.

The whole range of body experiences will link to the naming and use of parts of the body perhaps unknown to the child's limited experience. This awareness of the body will also link to the tactile senses of pain and temperature. It may help a child avoid a painful experience because of increased awareness of what is happening to a part of his body. For example, he may move his leg away from a prickly surface or move his body away from a hot radiator.

THE LINK TO A CHILD'S MOVEMENT PROGRAMME
The child usually has very limited physical movement or mobility. The use of a Tactile Programme may prompt him to

increase his movements in order to explore an object or move closer to an interesting tactile experience. The child may begin to use his mouth and tongue to explore, or to use a hand to touch an interesting texture.

These are significant movements for the child, and closely link several curriculum areas. For example, movement links to tactile experiences as the sense of movement gives the sensation of touch a richer experience. An example of this would be rolling a child over a variety of textured surfaces, thus integrating texture with movement.

2   Planning a Tactile Curriculum

SETTING YOUR AIMS

The main aim for the Tactile Curriculum should include the full development of a child's awareness of himself and his environment, through touch.

SETTING YOUR GOALS

The goals that are set for the Tactile Curriculum are not graduated or taught in a specific order. There is no developmental ladder to follow in working with the tactile sense. Everyone has a different level of response to touch or tactile experience. For example, some people cannot bear to stroke animals, or have wool next to their skin, while other people enjoy an icy shower or the feel of sandpaper. The very special child also has an individual response to touch and tactile experiences.

The goals that are set should not be set in isolation, but should be interlinked to other areas of the curriculum. For example, the goal of 'increasing fine motor movement' will link strongly with a child's Movement Programme. The touch and tactile experiences given to the child will further this objective. The goal of 'simple discrimination of touch experiences' will link to the work the child is doing in the area of choice and controlled movements.

The main goals may include some of the following:
— enjoyment,
— stimulation and awareness of tactile experiences,
— increased toleration of handling,
— awareness of contact,

— increase in fine motor movements,
— increase in gross motor movements,
— simple discrimination of tactile experiences,
— beginning of awareness of the characteristics of objects,
— awareness that touch has meaning,
— human contact through touch,
— increase in the use of the tongue and mouth to explore,
— beginning a touch/tactile memory bank.

PLANNING TACTILE UNITS

The main areas in which to begin a Tactile Programme are human touch, tactile objects, and tactile experiences. As the curriculum develops, these main areas can be broken down into more precise units. For example, the human touch area could include:

physical stimulation	multisensory touch
passive massage	active massage
nurture	finger and hand massage

These link closely to a child's Movement and Nurture Programme. Examples of two units—active and passive massage—are shown below. An individual programme is included in the Tactile Bank Section.

CURRICULUM DATA
Passive Massage

Curriculum area	:	Cognitive
Main objective	:	Sensory development
Stage	:	Tactile—passive massage
Resources	:	School curriculum and physiotherapist

1 Is indifferent to a range of passive massage.
2 Responds to foot massage.
3 Responds to hand massage.
4 Responds to shoulder massage.
5 Responds to lower back massage.
6 Responds to whole back massage.
7 Responds to limb massage.
8 Responds to head/face massage.
9 Responds to tummy massage.

10   Shows preference/dislike for a range of massage.
11   Shows own choice for certain massage.
12   Creates own massage—ie. rubs head, mouth, body, other.

CURRICULUM DATA
Active Massage

Curriculum area : Cognitive
Main objective : Sensory development
Stage : Tactile—active massage
Resources : School curriculum and physiotherapist

---

1   Is indifferent to a range of participatory massage.
2   Responds to a range of participatory massage, ie:
   a) finger play
   b) hand play
   c) feet to feet
   d) body to body
   e) pulling
   f) pushing
   g) stretching
   h) rolling
   i) swinging
   j) clapping
   k) other.
3   Shows preference/dislike for participatory massage.
4   Shows own choice for certain participatory massage.
5   Creates own particular massage:
   pushes, pulls, taps, hits, strokes, etc.
6   Other.

As well as the human touch stimulation, there are the areas of tactile objects and tactile experiences. These areas can be broken down into more precise units. For example, the tactile experience area could include:
   — sticky experiences,
   — air experiences,
   — vibratory experiences,
   — temperature experiences.

Examples of two units, sticky experiences and air stimulation, are illustrated next in this section. The Tactile Bank should hold a good range of resource materials for these areas.

CURRICULUM DATA
Sticky Experiences

Curriculum area   :   Cognitive
Main objective   :   Sensory development
Stage   :   Tactile—sticky experience
Resources   :   School curriculum

1 Is indifferent to a range of sticky materials.
2 Responds to a range of sticky materials.
3 Responds to a temperature change in sticky materials.
4 Shows preference/dislike for certain sticky materials.
5 Shows own choice for certain sticky materials.
6 Creates own stimulation using sticky materials, eg. mucus, dribbles, body waste, other.
7 Other.

CURRICULUM DATA
Air Experiences

Curriculum area   :   Cognitive
Main objective   :   Sensory development
Stage   :   Tactile—air stimulation
Resources   :   School curriculum

1 Is indifferent to physical stimulation using air.
2 Responds to a range of air stimulation on different parts of the body.
3 Responds to air movements on the body.
4 Responds to temperature change in air stimulation.
5 Shows preference/dislike for air stimulation.
6 Shows own choice of preferred air stimulation.
7 Creates own stimulation, eg. blows, sucks, waves arms, waves hands, other.
8 Other.

3   Linking the Child to the Tactile Curriculum

THE FAMILY CAN HELP

The child has most of his tactile experiences at home or in other caring environments. The family must continuously provide all the physical care he requires, and are acutely aware of how he reacts to handling, tactile experiences, and touch.

This information is invaluable in planning a Tactile Programme for the child and setting realistic goals. A simple sensory questionnaire should be completed by the family so that they are involved in the Tactile Programme at home, as well as at school (see Appendix A for a sample Sensory Questionnaire).

The family should be able to set tactile goals that *they* want the child to achieve. It may be a goal such as the child permitting his hair to be towelled dry, or the child tolerating lying on the grass in the garden.

A parent workshop in the sensory area of tactile experience will help to explain the aims of this particular area, and further involves the family.

'Tactile' homework can occasionally be sent home with the child (see Appendix B for a sample Homework Card). It may be a box of scratchy objects, or a request for the child occasionally to have a bowl of warm water in which to dabble his fingers. This is a good way of involving siblings, who usually have great fun with the 'tactile' homework and working/playing with their handicapped sibling.

THE SCHOOL CAN HELP

Information at school can be collected using a simple recording form (see Appendix C for Simple Recording Sheets). This form should be kept for a given period of time, during which a range of tactile experiences is presented. It will provide ongoing information of the child's progression in this area.

There is a range of reactions and non-reactions to be observed and used as the first steps in an individual Tactile Programme. Remember, some children may look as though they are rejecting a tactile experience, when they are actually enjoying it. Your overall knowledge of the child will guide you in interpretation.

The Table below lists typical reactions of rejection and acceptance, as a first guideline.

TABLE—TYPICAL REJECTION/ACCEPTANCE REACTIONS

Rejection Reaction	Acceptance Reaction
Reaction Range	Reaction Range
Is indifferent to a range of physical stimulation.	Is indifferent to a range of physical stimulation.
Rejects physical stimulation.	Accepts physical stimulation.
Reaction type	*Reaction type*
Startles	—
Stills	Stills
Facial expression changes	Facial expression changes
Shudders	Moves towards stimulation
Cries	Makes noises
Moans	Turns head to stimulation
Withdraws self	Moves arms or legs
Bangs head	Rolls over to stimulation
Rubs hands	Laughs and/or coos
Pushes away	Other
Other	

THE CHILD CAN HELP

The child 'helps' indirectly by providing the reactions observed. The observations that are made during a tactile session with individual children provide the foundation for the Tactile Programme for each child. The programme is related to the child and will meet only that child's particular needs. In other words, a general Tactile Curriculum cannot be applied universally to all children—each child is unique in this area.

To show how a child provides the information which forms the basis for an individual Tactile Programme, the following example illustrates a recording of a child's reactions to tactile experience. This example was derived from a complete set of recordings taken during a monthly period. From these recordings were derived the main objectives for the child, which were:

1 To find the kinds of stimuli which produce a positive response.
2 To increase tolerance of handling and being moved.

RECORDING FORM

Sensory Area: Tactile   Name: Timothy

Materials	Date	Exposure	Response	Comments
1) Feather duster		3 minutes to face, tummy, and arms.	Stilled. Smiled. Laughed when tummy was tickled.	Timothy kneeling on floor in free movement area, rubbing hands together.
2) Vibrator (low)		2 minutes, rested, repeated 2 minutes.	Moaned, rubbed head, hit back of hands, cried, made no attempt to move away. On repeat, rubbed head, moved legs away.	Timothy sitting in chair in table-top area, was approached from the front, letting him hear vibrator, first applied to legs.
3) Vibrating cushion (on 2)		5 minutes: 3 minutes, co-actively, 2 minutes on own.	Stilled, smiled, sat quite happily even when sat by himself.	Timothy sat between my legs on cushion, then on his own.
4) Sand		3 minutes, sand poured over his hands.	Threw himself back, stiffened, and cried.	Sitting on floor in 'messy' area.

OTHER PROFESSIONALS CAN HELP

Information should be requested from other professionals to help in planning the Tactile Programme. The multidisciplinary approach is of great importance.

The speech therapist can assist with desensitisation, icing and brushing procedures which can help with tactile tolerance in the facial and mouth areas.

The occupational therapist and physiotherapist can both work with the Tactile Programme in conjunction with the child's Movement Programme.

The aromatherapist and masseur from the local community can be involved in the specific areas of massage.

The local beautician, who is trained to work in the areas of hand and facial massage, may also be of help.

The different skills of these specialists may be of special application to individual children's programmes.

4 The Tactile Bank

WHAT IS A TACTILE BANK?

The Tactile Bank is one part of a sensory bank. It is a resource to complement the Tactile Curriculum. The Tactile Bank should provide a wide and stimulating range of tactile experiences. The bank is also used in conjunction with the child's Movement Programme.

BEGINNING A TACTILE BANK

An area of the room should be designated as the learning space for the tactile sense. The splash pool, sandpit, and the arts and crafts rooms could also be designated as tactile areas. This area could contain the following items:

— a lobster pot pen to fill with stimulating materials, eg. leaves, crumpled newspapers, etc.
— a small sand tray,
— a sit-in tray or bowl to fill with water/sawdust/sand/ cornflakes, etc.
— a small water tray,
— a messy waterproof mat to use for messy experiences, such as foam, paints, etc.

The tactile experience area should be near the sink or other washing-up area for easy cleaning.

It is advisable to have a suitable storage trolley or cupboard with appropriately-sized trays or boxes to hold the separate tactile experience materials. The containers should be childproof to prevent inquisitive children from using them unsupervised during the day. A source book of ideas for tactile touch experiences for each child should be available in the Tactile Bank.

The tactile materials should be checked regularly, and new materials added, as necessary.

SUGGESTIONS FOR SECTIONS IN A TACTILE BANK

Label each section to permit easy access for the particular tactile stimulation to be used in an observation session. Typical sections are shown below.

Main Tactile Sections
tactile movement   object touch   human touch

Tom and Amy feel, touch and explore a pile of feathers.

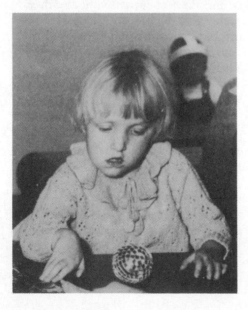

Amy examines the glittery mirror ball intently, before feeling it.

Other Tactile Sections
rough   smooth   soft touch   hard touch
scratchy touch   messy   woolly   liquids
feelie bags   hand-held touch   pounding materials
touch gloves   touch wall   contact programmes
skin ṣtimulation   facial stimulation   air stimulation
vibratory stimulation   temperature stimulation

Some tactile materials or ideas will be repeated in different sections. For example, sand could be in the messy, pouring materials, soft, and feelie bag sections. The objective being set for the child in each session would determine how the sand was used to test the objective in that session.

Below is a list of some tactile materials and ideas for use in some of the aforementioned tactile sections.

Messy Section
(used on floor, all over body, or for specific parts of the body, eg. feet in a bowl of materials, etc.)

corn flakes	flour
dried bread crumbs	dough
pasta	porridge oats (wet and dry)
felt pieces	washing up liquid
fingcr paint	pasce
gravel (coloured)	plasticine
salt (wet and dry)	shaving cream
sand (set and dry)	toothpaste
glycerine	vaseline

Skin Stimulation

hand cream	paint brush
fabric gloves	balloons
feathers	cotton-wool buds
feather duster	silky material

Air Stimulation

empty squeezy containers	balloons
fan	tubes to blow through
hair dryer	straws
hand-held battery fan	

Lobster Pot Play Pen or Pillow Case

filled with autumn leaves
polystyrene pieces
cloth

torn up newspaper
crinkly greaseproof
  paper
coloured balls

Hand Touch (to touch and hold)

nail brush
scrubbing brush
stones
blackboard rubber
fir cones
toothbrush
egg carton
rope

stone egg
textured animals
beanbag toys
candle
shells
combs
scouring pad
rubber squeaky toys

Soft Touch

velvet, wool materials
kapok
hops
fur
pot pourri
bottle teat

mop head
feathers
sponges
sand-filled stockings
lint
cotton-wool

Vibration

vibrating cushion
vibrator
battery fan
joke hand buzzer
vibro bubble
Pifco automatic foot spa
hand-held electric whisk
battery-powered
  toothbrush
hand-held car vacuum
  cleaner

facial massager
electric toothbrush
mechanical toys
drums
large cymbal
Gato drum (see Suppliers)

Massage

source book of ideas
  (opposite)

soapy water
oils

hand cream
fur gloves   soft towelling
baby powder   massage lotions, creams
                                      and aromatherapy oils
                                      (from Body Shop)

Pouring Materials (to pour over body)
aromatic oils   oils
dry sand   cereals/macaroni
lentils   peat
salt (being careful of any   beads
open cuts)   baking powder
gravel

Suppliers for Tactile Bank

Rompa, PO Box 5,   an extensive
Wheatbridge Road,   selection of
Chesterfield,   equipment
Derbyshire S40 2AE.

T F H   vibro bubble
76 Barracks Road,   hedgehog ball
Sandy Lane Industrial Estate,   flexi-rings
Stourport on Severn,   foam balls
Worcs. DY13 9EX.   large touch
                                    equipment

SOURCE BOOK OF TACTILE STIMULATION (MASSAGE AND TOUCH)
Sample Programme

Child   : Polly
Sensory area   : Tactile
Duration of
response   : Until child tolerates foot massage.
Aim   : A child who will tolerate human touch.
Objective   : Toleration of human touch on the feet.
Programme   : Feet massage.
Materials   : Oil, fur, silky fabric, soft towel.

1 Tell child what is going to happen and where.
2 Take to tactile area and tell child again what will be happening.
3 Make sure position is comfortable, preferrably lying on the floor.
4 Make sure materials are at hand.
5 Work slowly and softly, but with confidence.
6 Continually talk to and reassure the child.
7 Shoes and socks off.
8 Pat and stroke feet with hands. } Talk to child and
9 Pat and stroke feet with fur. } name foot parts
10 Pat and stroke feet with silk. } throughout the exercise.
11 Oil on hands.
12 Stroke feet.
13 Stroke toes.
14 Massage each part of the foot: toes, between toes, sole, heel, inner part of foot.
15 Dry feet with soft towel when finished.
16 Praise child and encourage co-operation.
17 When the child is used to the programme, let her feel *your* feet and help her to massage your feet or those of another child.

USING THE TACTILE BANK AND CURRICULUM WITH A CHILD

1 *Preparations beforehand*
— Refer to the child's records for any medical condition, allergies, or peculiarities, before commencing any new area of the Tactile Programme.
— Send home, and discuss with the family, the section on tactile stimulation in the Sensory Questionnaire.
— Have someone else record reactions, if possible, to enable an objective recording to be taken.
— Use a video camera for in-depth freeze-frame analysis of reactions.
— Decide the objective of the lesson beforehand, and *keep* to that objective.
— Check that all the materials are ready and available.

2   *The child in the tactile area*
— Talk to the child beforehand and let him know what is going to happen *before* you do anything.
— Take the child to the tactile area, explaining where you are going and what will happen.
— Check that the positioning of the child is comfortable for the child—and yourself.
— Check that the recording materials or video camera are on hand. Do not record every session, eg. perhaps one out of five, but record any significant points in between.
— Keep to the lesson objective.
— Prepare the tactile materials. Tell the child what tactile materials or experiences he will be given and be very encouraging to him.
— Allow the child to have plenty of time to experience the tactile stimulation.
— Observe and record while watching.
— Tell the child when the tactile session is finished, and praise his co-operation or achievement.
— Tell the child what is going to happen next and move him to the appropriate area.

3   *After the Tactile Session*
— Check recordings and plan the next step.
— Repeat and repeat tactile experiences, even if there is no reaction—there may be a reaction one day.
— Let the family know what progress is being made and occasionally send home 'fun' homework.
— Remember to include in the programme other people who are important to the child. Such people may have different approaches and different ideas to contribute to the value and range of the programme.
— Most importantly, try to *generalise* the tactile experiences in other situations. Talk to the child and remind him of the tactile situations as they arise during the day.
— Remember the importance of finger rhymes, nursery rhymes, and action rhymes which closely link together sound, words, movement, touch, and anticipation.

5   Tactile Curriculum—Action Checklist
1   Read relevant books and articles, and see relevant films.

2 Visit other schools and review their Tactile Banks and Curricula.
3 Begin collecting tactile materials to equip the Tactile Bank.
4 Plan a Tactile Curriculum with main aims, goals, and units.
5 Plan a recording system.
6 Involve parents and other people important to the child.
7 Plan and equip the Tactile Bank.
8 Keep materials in good condition and keep adding new tactile materials.
9 Evaluate the Tactile Curriculum and Tactile Bank regularly.

6 Helpful Books and Articles
Please refer to the main bibliography in Chapter 1 for general information that will help in developing a Sensory Curriculum and also help with recording and assessment.

Argyle, M. (1975). *Body Communication.* London: Methuen.
Argyle, M. (1979). *Person to Person—Ways of Communication.* Life Cycle Series. London: Harper and Row.
Browning, M. M. (1983). *Identifying the needs of Profoundly Mentally Handicapped Children.* Part 3—on functioning of the senses. Obtainable from: Publications Department, Jordanhill College of Education, Southbrae Drive, Glasgow.
Fast, J. (1971). *Body Language.* London: Pan Books.
Freeman, P. (1975). *Understanding the Deaf/Blind Child.* Chapter 11, tactile activities, programmes and training. London: Heinemann Medical Books.
Holle, B. (1976). *Motor Development in Children—Normal and Retarded.* Section on tactile senses. Oxford: Blackwell Scientific Publications.
Newson, E., and Hipgrave, T. (1982). *Getting through to Your Handicapped Child.* Chapter 7—Section on touch and feel. Cambridge University Press.
Schiff, W., and Foulke, E. (eds.) (1982). *Tactual Perception— A Source Book.* Cambridge University Press.
For further information on massage, see:
Leboyer, F. (1976). *Loving Hands.* Work on massage with young babies as used by Indian mothers. London: Fontana Books.

For further information on vibration, see: Niagra Therapy Research Project, Mary Sheridan Unit, Borocourt Hospital, Wyfold, Reading, Berks.

Byrne, D., and Stevens, C. (1980). 'Mentally handicapped children's responses to vibro-tactile and other stimuli as evidence for the existence of a sensory hierarchy', in *Apex—Journal of British Mentally Handicapped,* vol. 8, no 3, pp. 96-8.

Murphy, R. J., and Doughty, N. R. (1977). 'Establishment of controlled arm movement in profoundly retarded students using response contingent vibratory stimulation', in *American Journal of Mental Deficiency,* vol. 82, no. 2, pp. 212-16.

7 THE SENSE OF BODILY EXPERIENCE

Contents

1 Introduction

WHAT IS THE SENSE OF BODILY EXPERIENCE?
The sense of bodily experience is part of the somesthesia sense.
The somesthesia sense is divided into three parts, which link
together to form this sense. These are:

1) Kinesthetic sense—linking to: awareness of body
    (*sense organs in*   movement, perception
    the muscles,   of weight, awareness of
    tendons, and   body and limbs,
    joints)   laterality.

2) Visceral sense—linking to: hunger, nausea, and
                                    sexual feelings.
3) Vestibular sense—linking to: balance, body posture,
                                    sensation of rotation,
                                    and dizziness.

By the tension of some muscles, and the laxness of others, by
the positions of bones, tendons, and joints, we get a constant
stream of enormously detailed and useful information about
our posture and movements. This is achieved via the highly
complex sense organs in muscles, tendons, and joints.

The most important part of the somesthesia sense for the
very special child is the kinesthetic sense, or, as it is described in
this chapter, the sense of bodily experience.

THE LINK TO THE OTHER SENSES

The special child has a very limited capacity to explore his
environment, or even his own body. However, it is important
that he should learn through his own bodily experiences. He
should learn through 'doing', and not always by having
experience 'done' to him.

It may be that the adult has to hold, or manipulate, the child
through activities which involve a sense of movement, such as:

— being pushed on a swing,
— rolling over on the grass,
— going up and down on a seesaw,
— being tossed in a blanket,
— going for a ride on a trike,
— moving around the swimming pool,
— riding a horse.

Each of these types of movement will help enrich the child's
sense of bodily awareness and experience.

THE LINK TO A CHILD'S MOVEMENT PROGRAMME

This sense of bodily experience links closely to a child's
Movement Programme. It is fruitless to put a child through a
series of mechanical movements which do not link to the
senses, especially the sense of bodily experience. The movement
for the child then becomes more meaningful experience—
linking movement to bodily experience or using bodily
experience for movement.

2 Planning a Curriculum for the Sense of Bodily Experience

This curriculum *must* be part of a child's Movement Curriculum, and not used in isolation.

SETTING YOUR AIMS

The main aim of a sense of bodily experience/movement curriculum should be to develop a child's experience of movement by 'doing' and participating in bodily experiences.

SETTING YOUR GOALS

It is difficult to set a wide variety of goals in this area. It should be closely linked to a child's Movement Programme and the goals set for a child in this area. The sense of bodily experience should be an integral part of any meaningful movement for the child.

The goals may include:
— enjoyment and fun,
— anticipation,
— increased toleration of handling,
— increased toleration of new movement experiences,
— increase in bodily awareness,
— awareness of limbs,
— beginning of perception of body weight,
— beginning of understanding movement,
— increased awareness of movement.

One or two of these goals would be linked to goals set for a child in his Movement Programme.

Because it is difficult to set goals, the sense of bodily movement is also very hard to assess or evaluate. Her close knowledge of the child and his reactions to movement experiences will give the teacher some means of evaluating his understanding of bodily experiences. However, it is an area that cannot be neatly recorded or assessed.

PLANNING CURRICULUM UNITS

There is a variety of areas to consider when planning curriculum units in the sense of bodily experience. These may include:
— the using of muscles, joints and limbs,
— use of body weight,

— body awareness,
— the tension and relaxation of the body,
— movement in space.

It must be stressed that the development of these units would be in conjunction with the Movement Programme and with movement experts. Trained help should be requested from the physiotherapist, occupational therapist, movement therapist and remedial gymnast. If help is not available from any source, then it is advisable to request the Headteacher to seek some expert advice.

An example of a sense of bodily experience unit follows. As has already been stated, it is a difficult area to capture on paper and is open to wide interpretation.

CURRICULUM DATA
Sense of Bodily Movement

Curriculum area	:	Cognitive
Main objective	:	Sensory development
Stage	:	Sense of bodily movement—movement in space
Resources	:	School curriculum, movement programme, occupational therapist, physiotherapist, movement therapist, remedial gymnast.

---

1 Shows awareness of movement through space, eg. being carried to a space for an activity.
2 Uses parts of the body, other than hands, to touch an object, eg. the head, tongue, back, limbs, etc.
3 Uses spasms to stretch limbs on body to explore immediate surroundings.
4 Uses combined senses—smell, taste, hearing—to gain knowledge of where the child is, eg. smell of dinner, rattle of plates in dining hall.
5 Shows awareness by facial expression of absence of familiar person.
6 Shows awareness of entry of familiar person, by change of activity, eg. stilling, spasmodic movement of limbs and body, eye contact, sounds, etc.

7   Shows awareness of direction by eye-pointing.
8   Has an awareness of his body in relationship to his moving limbs.

___

3   Linking the Child to the Sense of Bodily Experience Curriculum

THE FAMILY CAN HELP

The very special child has many bodily experiences at home or in his other caring environment. Information provided from the home is a good basis on which to begin to build a set of experiences to help a child to develop his sense of bodily experience.

A simple sensory questionnaire could be completed by the family so that they are involved in the bodily experience programme at home, as well as at school. (See Appendix A for a sample Sensory Questionnaire).

A parent workshop in the sense of bodily experience, linked closely to a child's Movement Programme, will further explain the aims of this particular area and further involve the family. 'Bodily experience' homework can be occasionally sent home for the child, linked to his Movement Programme.

Families usually rise to the challenge—especially siblings. Homework may be a request for the child to be gently tossed in a blanket, or swung around in an adult's arms. See Appendix B for a sample Homework Card.

THE SCHOOL CAN HELP

Information at school can be collected by recording the range of bodily experience which the child has received. A simple recording form can be used, but it must be remembered that it is a very difficult area in which to record objectively. (See Appendix C for Simple Recording Sheets). However, it is important to *try* to record all the different bodily experiences a child receives at school.

THE CHILD CAN HELP

The child 'helps' through the teacher's observations of him in a series of bodily experience situations. These observations of bodily experience will be an integral part of the observations of the child and his movements.

Some observations:

Child	Event	Reaction
William	Being tossed in a blanket.	Shrieked and laughed, began to anticipate each toss.
	Rolled down small hillock.	Began to try to roll himself himself when downhill momentum ceased.
	Held by an adult and bounced on a trampoline	Shrieked and held breath, began to push feet down when movement stopped.

These observations would be useful for planning the child's Movement Programme and also for new steps in the Cognitive Programme.

OTHER PROFESSIONALS CAN HELP

It is vital to involve other professionals in the area of sense of bodily experience. The physiotherapist, occupational therapist, movement specialist, and remedial gymnast can all contribute and help. The difficulty of identifying, and of monitoring, a child's development of a sense of bodily experience, as seen in the examples given, requires an integrated multidisciplinary approach.

4   Resources for the Sense of Bodily Experience

The sense of bodily experience for a child does not fit conveniently into a sense bank. However, a sense of bodily movement Resource can relate to the wealth of movement in the Movement Curriculum for each child. This Resource can also hold a collection of experiences that could encourage development of the child's sense of bodily experience.

In other words, the sense of bodily experience Resource would contain:

—   a Resource book of ideas,
—   a Resource book noting apparatus or places to promote a sense of bodily experience,
—   the school Movement Curriculum, for reference.

To begin this Resource, an area of the classroom or school can be designated as a space for the promotion of the sense of bodily experience. It may well be that many of these experiences will happen in other areas, such as outside, in a rumpus room, in the local park, or in the school hall. Other activities, such as riding, swimming or sailing, could also be used for the stimulation of the sense of bodily experience. These Resource areas would be noted in the Resources Files for the sense of bodily experience 'bank'.

Here are some ideas for apparatus that could be used to promote a sense of bodily experience:

large inflatables	play pen full of balls
a hammock	inclining boards
a blanket	wobbly board
lilo	thick sponge mat
water bed	rocking horse
trampoline	crazy chickens
rompa large ball	swings
large inner tubes	slides
pillows	

Simon enjoys a bodily movement experience in the ball pool.

But, above all else, the MOST IMPORTANT resource in this area is HUMAN CONTACT—in other words, HUMANS who:

hug	swim	ride	hop	skip
swing	roll	swirl	run	gallop
march	lift	whirl	dance	jump

with the child, encouraging the child to respond with his own movements.

Useful Suppliers of Material

Toys for the Handicapped, 76 Barracks Road, Stourport on Severn, Worcs DY13 9QB.   coracle swing, bolster swing, leaf chain, giant top, water bed, trampolines, swinging hammock, cord hammock.

5   Sense of Bodily Experience Curriculum—Action Checklist
1   Read relevant books and articles, and see relevant films.
2   Visit other schools and review their work on the sense of bodily experience.
3   Plan a Sense of Bodily Experience Curriculum in conjunction with the Movement Curriculum.
4   Involve the family and other people who are important to the child.
5   Plan a Resource File to promote the sense of bodily experience.
6   Keep adding new experiences to the Resource File.
7   Evaluate the Sense of Bodily Experience Curriculum regularly.

6   Helpful Books and Articles
Please refer to the main bibliography in Chapter 1 for general information that will help in developing a sensory curriculum, and also with recording and assessment.

Auxter, D. (1971). 'Motor Skill Development in the Profoundly Retarded', in *Training School Bulletin,* no. 68, pp. 5-9
Browning, M. M. *et al.* (1983). *Identifying the Needs of Profoundly Mentally Handicapped Children.* Section Three—on kinesthetic or proprioceptive sense. Obtainable from: Publications Department, Jordanhill College of Education, Southbrae Drive, Glasgow G13 1PP.
Cotton, E. *The Basic Motor Pattern.* Obtainable from: The

Spastics Society, 12 Park Crescent, London W1N 4EQ.

Cotton, E. *The Hand as a Guide to Learning.* Obtainable from: The Spastics Society, 12 Park Crescent, London W1N 4EQ.

Finnie, R. (1974). *Handling the Young Cerebral Palsied Child at Home.* London: Heinemann Medical Books.

Gilroy, P. *Kids in Motion: Early Childhood Movement.* Winslow Press.

Gilroy, P. *Kids in Action: Developing Body Awareness in Young Children.* Winslow Press.

Golding, R., and Goldsmith, L. (1986). *The Caring Person's Guide to Handling the Severely Multiply Handicapped.* London: Macmillan.

Groves, L. (1979). *Physical Education for Special Needs* (paperback). Cambridge University Press.

Holle, B. (1976). *Motor Development in Children Normal and Retarded.* Section on the kinesthetic sense. Oxford: Blackwell Scientific Publications.

Law, I. H., and Suckling, M. H. (1983). *Handling When Children are Profoundly Handicapped.* Obtainable from: Publications Department, Jordanhill College of Education, Southbrae Drive, Glasgow G13 1PP.

McCarthy, C., and Sheehy, A. *All About Me: Activities for Self-Awareness.* Winslow Press.

Mira, M. (1977). 'Tracking the Motor Behaviour Development of Multiply Handicapped Infants', in *Mental Retardation,* vol. 15, no. 3, pp. 32-7.

Presland, J. L. (1982). *Paths to Mobility in 'Special Care'.* A guide to teaching gross motor skills to very handicapped children. Obtainable from: British Institute of Mental Handicap, Wolverhampton Road, Kidderminster, Worcs.

Upton, G. (1979). *Physical and Creative Activities for the Mentally Handicapped.* Cambridge University Press.

Vernon, M. D. (1970). *Perception through Experience* (includes section on the perception of movement). London: Methuen.

Webb, R. C. (1969). 'Sensory Motor Training of the Profoundly Retarded', in *The American Journal of Mental Deficiency* vol. 74, pp. 283-95.

Wyman, R. (1986). *Multiply Handicapped Children.* (Contains chapters on motor skills and making sense of a child's world.) London: Souvenir Press.

8 THE MULTISENSORY APPROACH—USING ALL THE SENSES SIMULTANEOUSLY

Contents

1   Introduction

WHAT IS A MULTISENSORY APPROACH?

A multisensory approach aims to use all the child's senses to break through the barrier of a child's handicap and communicate with the child. *Anita Royall*

'Communication' means the giving or receiving of information. Communication occurs via interactions between a child and the child's partner, using many senses—hence the Multisensory Approach.

Communication between the special child and his partner is an interaction of a very close and special kind. The communication is on a simple level, ie. the child's level, not a level imposed on the child by an adult. The child is therefore free to use his own means of communication, using all his senses, to make the communication meaningful. The child is able to succeed even though no conventional means of communication is used. The partner must learn the skill of observing and understanding how the child is using his senses to communicate.

Imagine a very special child using just two senses to explore and communicate. The Table opposite lists some of the experiences he may use with his partner for communication, using smell and touch.

The most important factor in the Multisensory Approach is that all the senses are used and it is not seen in isolation from the rest of the curriculum. It reflects all the child's sensory learning in one session and helps him to begin to generalise his sensory learning from individual sensory sessions. This multisensory generalisation will also be encountered in the child's environment in areas such as feeding or being changed.

THE LINK TO THE SENSES

The multisensory experience draws from all the senses, combining their input into an interaction meaningful to the child. The sensory curriculum used for the child is taught in a variety of sensory situations and with individual objectives for

TABLE—EXAMPLES OF COMMUNICATION VIA SMELL AND TOUCH

Communication via Sense of Smell

From the partner	*From the environment*
smell of skin	dusty floor smell
smell of hair, perfume, deodorant, powder	polish smell
smell of sweat	disinfectant smell
mouth smell	rubber mat smell
hands smell	room smell
feet smell	air freshener smell
clothes smell	smell of someone nearby
shoes and socks smell	

Communication via Sense of Touch

From the partner	*From the environment*
rough sweater	hard floor
cotton shirt	soft, bouncing mat
a necklace, bracelet, or ring	cold mat
buttons, buckles, zip	warm floor
textures of skin	smooth surface
textures of hair, bristles	touch of strings, eg. guitar
feel of fingers	feel of an accordion
warm breath	vibrating drum
hands tapping	warm air
hands pushing	cold draughts
hands pulling	moving over a surface
body enclosing	Movements:
moving lips	fast, slow, bumpy, soft, jerky, roly-poly, up and down, and all movements to create new touches.
humming throat	

each sense. These single sensory skills must be generalised by the child to provide a meaningful learning experience. The Multisensory Approach provides a means for the child to begin to generalise and to use this sensory learning.

THE LINK TO THE OVERALL CURRICULUM

The Multisensory Approach encapsulates all the learning experiences of the child, using not only the senses, but the whole range of skills being developed in the overall curriculum. We list here some of the areas that will be utilised in the Multisensory Approach. Most of the objectives set in these areas can be met in the multisensory therapy sessions:

Communication	Behavioural Change
Movement	Life Skills
Cognitive	Expressive Arts
Emotions	Sensory

THE LINK WITH THE FAMILY

The family, or other caring environment, is the most important part of any child's life—even more so with the very special child. The family must remain constant throughout the child's life. There is no realistic independence in sight for the very special child: the family must always support.

The family also offers the closest, warmest and most loving experience for the child, providing care and love throughout his life and the strongest emotional bonds. The child trusts the family more than any outsider.

The Multisensory Approach helps open the door, during the school day, to permit this warm trust to be used in opening up learning experiences for the child. The family can provide the best, most loving partner to expand the child's multisensory awareness and experiences.

Once a family member is committed to a regular, weekly multisensory session, then a very strong link can be established with the whole family. School and home share a mutual goal and mutual experiences. It is usually the mother who participates, but other family members can also help, with perhaps siblings, a grandparent, or dad attending occasional sessions.

The times before and after sessions are an ideal opportunity for direct contact and support for both home and school. Trust is gradually built up over the sessions and results in strong, honest relationships between home and school.

THE LINK TO OTHER PROFESSIONALS
Other professionals can readily be included in the planning of Multisensory sessions. Many of the single objectives they have been working on individually with the child can be met in the sessions, which enable them to evaluate how far their own particular objectives for a child are being generalised into other situations.

These sessions also create a very opportune time to see a family member at school on a regular basis. This meeting can be arranged after a multisensory session, and can give the professional an additional opportunity for developing a working relationship with the family.

THE LINK TO THE COMMUNITY
Sometimes, circumstances prevent a family member from helping in the multisensory sessions. School staff can be used in the sessions instead, or a volunteer from the community.

If outside volunteers are used, they must commit themselves to regular ongoing multisensory sessions with a child. The matching of a volunteer with a particular child is very important: a trusting and loving bond has to be established. It obviously helps if there is an initial liking on both sides, so that the volunteer will become a friend of the child. Friends are few and far between for the very special child—but greatly valued.

2 Developing a Multisensory Approach at Wren Spinney School, 1983

Wren Spinney School began to explore the possibilities of a Multisensory Approach to the very special child more than five years ago. This section describes the evolution of this approach at the school over a period of two years.

THE REASONS FOR PLANNING A MULTISENSORY APPROACH AT WREN SPINNEY SCHOOL
There were many reasons for beginning to plan a Multisensory Approach at Wren Spinney School:

(a)   There was no physiotherapy or occupational therapy available for any of the children. Staff felt that this lack of provision was of great harm to each child, and that some form of regular general movement could be used with the children for their benefit. The staff did not have the expertise to solve many of the problems posed by the multiply physically handicapped children, but they could help in this way at least.

(b)   Music was available for the children through the music teacher, who saw them three or four times a week. However, staff felt that the level of involvement in the music session was low, and that such sessions were better suited to the more able children in the school.

(c)   The Communication Curriculum was being devised for the school as a whole, and staff felt that the very special children's communication ability ended where the school programme began. Their level of communication was as simple as startling at sounds, or smiling—and no more.

(d)   Parents were keen to help at the school, but the traditional role of a parent helper was hard to fill because of their children's handicaps.

(e)   A Sensory Curriculum was being devised for the children, but it was felt that the integration of the senses was essential in the success of such a curriculum. The senses should not be isolated or treated separately.

(f)   There were many offers of volunteer help to the school. Using volunteers in a positive constructive way would be of benefit both to the school and the volunteers.

BEGINNING THE MULTISENSORY APPROACH

Wren Spinney School now began to tackle the planning for the Multisensory Approach in the following way:

—   Staff invited an out-of-county school to visit for the day to show how that school used music and movement therapy with its very special children. Families, other professionals and school staff were invited to watch the session, join in, and discuss the approach.

—   The session was video-recorded to allow further discussion.

— It was decided that a Multisensory Approach to meet the particular needs of the children at Wren Spinney School had to be devised—specifically to meet the unique requirements of each child.

Over the next six months, the following took place:

— Staff, including the Headteacher, worked as a team, discussing and planning the steps to be taken.

— The team viewed the video of the visiting school's sessions.

— Books and articles of relevance to the multisensory area were located (see the bibliography for this chapter, p. 176).

— The team looked at the work of Veronica Sherbourne, who stresses relationships, trust and care in her work with children with severe learning difficulties (see bibliography for this chapter).

— The new (proposed) approach was discussed with the music teacher, enlisting his help and co-operation in planning the songs, music and instruments. He would also take on the responsibility of leading the group musically in the sessions.

— Staff went on a variety of courses concerning physiotherapy, to gain some basic knowledge of movement.

— Unofficial approaches were made to several friendly physiotherapists for general advice on a child, in relationship to movement.

— Families were informed of how the planning was progressing and asked to help, if they so wished. *No* pressure was placed on the families to ensure that there would be no guilt feelings if they decided not to participate.

— Suitable volunteers were arranged for individual children.

— A time was arranged for full use of the hall facilities at the school.

— Comfortable mats were made available for the children and their partners to sit on during the sessions in the hall.

— The hall was set out and cleared away for each session by the school caretaker.

THE FIRST SESSIONS

The first sessions of a Multisensory Programme are difficult and stilted. This is because the group has to get used to each other, both adults and children. Here are some of the problems encountered at the start of the programme implemented at Wren Spinney School.

— No one quite knew what was going to happen and we all felt rather self-conscious.
— One or two children cried and were distressed for the first few weeks and did NOT want to join in.
— Some adults FELT like crying because they did not feel comfortable with the child or the situation.
— The tempo of the music was far too quick, with no time to move the children who had stiff limbs, and no interlude between songs.
— No one know all the words to the songs, or the tunes, or had the courage to sing clearly.
— Some movements proved too difficult—for example, rolling the child up into an adult's arms and down again.
— The body part section left a lot to the adults' imagination. This led to quite a lot of observing of other adults—surreptitiously!
— Teachers were seen to make mistakes and this was hard for some adults to accept.
— There was no sense of humour if things were wrong, which is essential in a working situation.

After about a month, however, the confidence of the group improved. A team spirit developed and everyone became more at ease. The crying children had stopped objecting and the adults now moved confidently and with assurance. Problems, such as movements which were too difficult for the children to execute, or too quick a tempo, were resolved.

While the group became confident, they were also sensitive to new adults and children attending the sessions, giving them warm support.

So it is important to remember that, when planning a Multisensory Approach, the first sessions will be far from perfect. But, if patience and time are given to the group, then they will begin to form a working group of great potential.

ONGOING DEVELOPMENTS IN THE MULTISENSORY APPROACH

There have been on-going developments in the Multisensory group work at Wren Spinney School. This is inevitable, and is also a good indication of how the group is developing and requiring more stimulation to help learning. Programme development has occurred to meet the demands of the children, who have moved on despite their handicaps.

Here are some of the changes that have taken place over a two-year period:

— introduction of new musical instruments,
— introduction of group work,
— introduction of finger work,
— introduction of social games,
— inclusion of the group in a session with more able children.

These changes did not all happen at once, but were planned, tried, and accepted or rejected, over months. Some programme areas became obsolete, or were moved to other areas of the curriculum. For example, the body sounds are now in the sound sessions in the classroom.

3 Planning the Multisensory Approach

SETTING YOUR AIMS

The main aim of a Multisensory Approach is to combine the use of all the senses to allow communication for the very special child.

SETTING YOUR GOALS

The goals that are set for the Multisensory Curriculum should not be seen as either graduated or isolated steps. They must be part of a combined sensory approach for the child. They cannot be seen as a developmental set of goals, but as targets that incorporate goals from other areas of the curriculum. For example, the goal of 'increased tolerance to handling' will be included in most of the main areas of the curriculum for the very special child.

The main goals may include some of the following:
— enjoyment and fun,
— combined stimulation of all senses,
— encouragement of the child to use his senses,
— increased toleration of handling,
— increased toleration of new experiences,
— increase in movement,
— increase in body awareness,
— simple discrimination,
— beginning of communication,
— increase in facial expression,
— beginning to learn how to make friends,
— spontaneity of choice,
— learning to gain information from the environment,
— appreciation of music,
— beginning to understand time,
— anticipation.

Only one or two of these main goals would be selected for an individual child.

4   The Content of a Multisensory Programme

PLANNING MULTISENSORY UNITS
The main areas of the Multisensory Approach *must come directly* from the unique requirements of the group of children involved in the sessions. The units cannot be borrowed from another group, because each group is unique in its set-up, composition, and requirements.

MUSICAL CONTENT OF THE MULTISENSORY PROGRAMME
There is a variety of reasons why music plays such an important part in the Multisensory Approach:
— it is enjoyable,
— it holds the session together,
— it links each unit,
— it is open ended and open to interpretation,
— it has memory associations,
— it relaxes,
— it is structured,
— it gives sense to time,
— it is vibratory,

— it decides the tempo of a session,

— it helps the mood of the group.

The best person to use for music content is someone who is versatile, flexible, and sensitive to the requirements of the group. It does not matter which musical instrument is used, flute, accordion, and guitar having all been successfully used in sessions.

However, if such a person is not available, it is possible to use simple percussion instruments, accompanied by the human voice. Each percussion sound could link to a movement, just as a sound links to a body part in the multisensory session. It is more difficult to use taped music, because the tape recorder is insensitive to the mood of the group or the pace of a session.

It may be possible to locate a volunteer in the community who is willing to contribute musically to the session on a regular basis.

The actual music for the sessions can be evolved with the help of a musical specialist. Again, the needs of the group of children dictate the music. A group of stiff, non-ambulant children may find it difficult to move to very fast music. A group of overactive, energetic children may find it hard to work slowly and quietly with very slow, ponderous music.

Some of the tunes can be already known to the children, such as nursery rhymes or popular songs. This approach is useful if there is no music specialist to help in the planning of the music. The words of the songs should match the movements of the children. This means that if a favourite tune or rhyme is used, then a new set of words, relevant to the child's movements, is required.

The music for the body sounds is very simple, ie. linking a musical sound to a body part. There are also body sounds to be explored such as chest noises, cheek noises, or finger clicking. Some examples of suitable words and music will be found in the books listed at the end of this chapter.

TOUCH AND HANDLING IN THE MULTISENSORY PROGRAMME

The Multisensory Approach demands closeness of touch and contact between child and partner. The quality of the touch can dictate the success or failure of the session and of the relationship. This is why there must be a careful matching of child to partner, bearing in mind the child's temperament, movements, and susceptibility to touch.

For example, on one occasion, a mother found it hard to touch and work with her own, very overactive child. So during sessions, she partnered a floppy, inactive child, and worked well with her. Her child was in turn partnered with a very lively and robust volunteer. The volunteer enjoyed the child's activity and was able to channel his energy in parallel with her own.

When the partners remain constant, there is the opportunity to develop fully the quality of touch contact. This helps the relationship to grow, and it also transfers to the classroom, when the partner nurtures the child before and after the session.

The touch a child receives indicates the feeling of the partner, and the partner must be aware of the importance of her handling of a child. It reflects her mood to the child who knows if the partner is pleased, tolerant, firm, or in a bad temper. Even if the child can see a face, he may be unable to make sense of what the face is saying. He may also be unable to interpret non-verbal signals. It is very easy to smile and say nice words, whereas an abrupt movement reflects the true feelings of the speaker.

The touch and handling of a child will be reflected in the words used with him. He should be talked to all the time, encouraged, and helped to understand the handling he is receiving.

The words of the songs should also reflect the touch and handling the child receives. For example:
— 'Stretch your legs and stretch again.'
— 'Hands go round and round and round.'
— 'Feet go tap, tap, tap . . .'

Finally, it is important to make sure that the child is allowed to hug and touch his partner. It may be that he will have to be manipulated into the position required, but he will learn from touching and feeling the partner's head, hair, hands and body. They will begin to feel closer and more intimate in this sharing of touch.

THE RANGE OF TOUCH AND TACTILE STIMULATION
There is a varied range of touch and tactile stimulation that can be used during the multisensory sessions. The broader the

range offered, the greater the opportunity for the child to receive a touch sensation not previously experienced.

Here are some examples of the range of tactile stimulations possible:

Try:	tapping
	pinching (gently!)
	stroking
	tapping and strumming
	drumming a beat
Use:	fingertips
	palm
	side of hand
	thumb and forefinger
Go:	slowly
	quickly
	intermittently
	rhythmically
With:	light touch
	firm touch
	alternating light and firm touch

Also, encourage the child to do these actions to you, moulding his hands, if necessary.

MOVEMENT IN THE MULTISENSORY PROGRAMME

Other professionals, such as the physiotherapist and occupational therapist, can help in planning the range of movements which will be of benefit to the group. If their expertise is not available, it is worthwhile to request help from various societies, some of which are listed in the final section of the chapter.

The needs of the group of children who are to use the multisensory sessions will indicate the range of movements to be undertaken. The group may be mobile, or unable to move at all. It is difficult to have a mixed group of mobile and immobile children, as the session may then become too volatile to handle. In this case, the session should be given in two parts to meet the differing needs of the two groups. It may be that the movements of behaviourally disturbed or hyperactive children require a ratio of two partners per child, or a different session time.

LINKING MOVEMENTS WITH SOUND AND WORDS

Once the range of movement has been decided, the individual movements can be linked to words and sounds.

The movements of the whole body need to be taken into account and matched with appropriate music. Here is an example of the range of movements, linked to sound and music, for a very mobile group of children:

— arms in the air and shake,
— elbows in and out,
— head around and around,
— back against back,
— shoulders up and down,
— swinging arms,
— marching,
— on tiptoes,
— knees up and down,
— rotating trunk,
— dancing fingertips,
— roly polys.

Each movement should be linked to a tune and an appropriate lyric.

EVOLVING AN ONGOING MULTISENSORY APPROACH

As in all areas of the curriculum, the Multisensory Approach should be ongoing and open to change. This implies that it will develop further to meet the evolving requirements of the group. Change is not readily accepted by the very special child and needs to be undertaken slowly and carefully. The whole group needs time to assimilate change.

There are many areas in the Multisensory Approach that may require changes, each unique to a particular group of children and school. The important point is that everyone involved should be aware of, and observant of, the need for change, in order to accommodate new factors.

ADDITIONS TO THE ORIGINAL SESSIONS

Here are some examples of changes that could be used in an evolving approach.

— The group may evolve to include group work, the child joining with his partner in a whole group for part of the session. The group may work in a close-knit circle, with adults forming the outer circle, and children supported in an inner circle.

— The child and partner may work in a foursome, in order to begin to develop a new relationship with new people. It is the beginning of expanding a child's horizons beyond just himself and his partner. The child has derived the confidence to do this from working with the partner.

— The use of materials other than musical instruments may be introduced into sessions, although not all ideas would be used at once. Here are some suggestions:

* A long strip of material can be used for everyone to hold while joining in the rocking songs. This will help to introduce a 'group' feeling as all members of the group hold on to the material and rock or sway together to the music.

*Use a handkerchief or scarf for group work on a 'peek-a-boo' theme. There is an added anticipation aimed at the child who is hidden for a few moments during the song.

*Use long coloured streamers to wave during a song or piece of music. Shiny metallic streamers add a new visual dimension to the song.

*Tinsel on everyone's hands or feet can emphasise their individual movements as well as enhancing the visual impact of the group's movements as a whole.

*Bells can be attached to the wrists to help strengthen the link between movement and sound.

*Use a parachute or other large piece of material to work *under*, for a change of experience.

— Expand the use and range of musical instruments, perhaps incorporating percussion.

— There may be a need for the group to expand and move into the area of added stimulation available from working with a group of more able children.

— Older pupils in the school may be brought into the sessions to meet some of *their* needs as well as those of the younger children. This would be very opportune if there was a school policy to incorporate the very special adolescent into the main school and not in a separate unit or class.

— The whole group could be involved in planning and evaluating any new changes in the Multisensory Approach. They will have the confidence to do this as the sessions progress.

The Multisensory Approach can be utilised in the general areas of a child's work at school. The addition of a sensory clue or aid will help the child by giving him an extra chance of making sense of his experiences. For example, the child may be given a scented bar of soap to hold as he is encouraged to look for his hands. The smell may encourage a movement of the hand towards the head.

Similarly, if the child enjoys the songs used in a multisensory session, then the same songs may be used as help in other areas. For example, sing the words of the songs linked to leg movements as the child's legs are moved during changing or during exercises.

5 Research into the Multisensory Sessions at Wren Spinney School

[The following section was taken, with permission, from *Collaboration between Parents and Special School*, 1984, pp. 68-77, an unpublished dissertation by Andrea Hallman for the University of Leicester.]

Introduction—My Reasons for Choosing This Area of Research
As part of my study of collaboration between parents and special schools, I have made several visits to Wren Spinney School in Northamptonshire. The school involves, and works with, parents in a variety of different ways. Of particular interest to me were the weekly Multisensory Therapy Sessions, where members of staff and parents worked together with a group of profoundly multi-handicapped children.

I decided to set aside a small section of my study to look at the sessions from the parents' point of view. I wrote to the parents concerned and asked them if they would spend some time after one of the therapy sessions discussing what they considered to be the benefits of their involvement in this school-based programme.

The findings of my discussion with the parents are set out later in the study.

Multisensory Therapy—Wren Spinney School
Wren Spinney School is a Northamptonshire Special School for pupils with severe to profound learning difficulties from the age of two. The school is about two and a half years old and presently has 53 pupils on its roll. Children attending the school have a wide range of special needs, and the staff are continually assessing and adapting the curriculum to suit the pupils.

Some eighteen months ago, the school decided to review the curriculum it provided for ten of its pupils who were profoundly multi-handicapped. After considerable discussion and work, a structure was developed based on the five senses, and the classroom for these children subsequently divided into specific teaching areas, for ease and efficiency.

As well as dealing with the five senses individually, the staff felt that there should be an area of the curriculum which dealt with the senses together—a multisensory element. The school's music teacher and the homebase teacher for the profoundly multi-handicapped, together with the Headteacher, devised a programme of multisensory therapy involving music, movement of the children's limbs, and singing, thus linking words to actions and body parts.

It (the multisensory session) was designed to take place weekly for 40 minutes, and, because of the acute levels of handicap involved, would require a number of adults to work on a one-to-one basis with each child. The music teacher would play instruments and, along with the class teacher, would lead the other adults involved in a programme of singing and interacting with the children.

The therapy sessions began, and as many staff as were available were involved in order to implement this multisensory approach to the children's education. For the first week or so the music teacher, the class teacher, the Headteacher, the school secretary, nursery nurses, and anyone else available, were used in order to run the sessions. Obviously this was a drain on staffing and sometimes, if enough staff were not available, it meant that one adult had to work with two children; not the ideal situation, as the therapy was designed for a one-to-one, ongoing working relationship.

The school had already established very good relationships with the parents of its pupils, and so a natural progression was to informally ask the parents of the children concerned if they would like to help out in the therapy sessions. The class teacher asked parents as she saw them, being careful not to pressurise the parents into feeling obligated to help. The response was very good, and, over the past 18 months, there has been an average of six parents in a group regularly helping out in the weekly sessions. Although mostly mothers, the group did temporarily include an unemployed father who regularly came into school to help out, until he found another job.

Parents arrive, usually in good time for the session, and are involved with their child for the duration of the therapy. The parents, along with the staff, work together seated on PE mats. The sessions are designed in such a way as to allow any newcomers to pick up the songs and movements very easily indeed. A list of songs and actions is displayed for the adults to read and there is no shortage of help and support from the more experienced members of the group. The sessions are conducted in a friendly and informal way, and parents and staff generally address each other on first name terms.

The sessions, it is interesting to note, have evolved and changed continuously since they first began some 18 months ago. This change and development is a *fundamental* part of the sessions, and the Headteacher is very careful to point this out. Already the sessions have adopted a 'group-work' element, as well as the one-to-one work which forms a large part of the 40-minute period.

Invitation to Parents to Discuss the Multisensory Sessions
A letter was devised and sent to those parents who were coming regularly to the multisensory therapy sessions. The letter stated that I would very much like to know what the parent considered to be the benefits of this kind of collaboration. To that end, I hoped that the parent would be willing to help me

with my study after one of the therapy sessions, by attending a short interview in the Parents' Room. I stated that the meeting would only last about 15 minutes, and that we would provide a cup of coffee to make the task a little more enjoyable.

I also prepared a simple question sheet, asking the parent to write down three ways in which either she or her child benefited from involvement in this programme.

Findings of Discussion Session
I arrived at Wren Spinney School and 'set up' in the Parents' Room. I had prepared question sheets, which I hoped would stimulate conversation, and had arranged to provide coffee for the parents. One mother could not stay behind to talk to me after the therapy session because she had to pick up another of her children from school. She did, however, take the time to come and talk to me for a few minutes.

After the therapy session, four mothers came into the Parents' Room to talk to me and altogether they spent about 20 minutes writing and discussing the value of their involvement in the sessions.

The points brought up in the discussion were as follows:
a)   Four of the five mothers who spoke to me told me that they felt that the Multisensory Therapy was an *extremely* important element of their children's education. They felt that music was vitally important for the profoundly multi-handicapped and recognised their own value in providing the necessary level of staffing for such a project.

b)   All of the mothers mentioned that the therapy provided a transferable learning situation and four of the mothers frequently used the songs and actions of the therapy sessions in unstructured situations at home. One mother expressed very strongly the value she saw in singing to her child and all of the mothers agreed that activities which involved music reinforced their children's learning. 'I think it is important as we sing and do the same things each time. This routine educates the children as they associate tunes and words with different actions. Repetitions of tunes, etc., can improve their limited memories.' Another mother commented on the fact that the therapy sessions had 'given her ideas as to what to do with him'.

c)   The opportunity of visiting school was singled out as being very beneficial. Two mothers contrasted and compared 'normal' children and their own. The mothers felt that there needed to be contact between parents and special schools because the children cannot communicate about their (school) experiences as 'normal' children can. The mothers valued their involvement in the therapy sessions and felt that it gave them some insight into the education which the school was providing for their children.

d)   It was mentioned by two of the mothers that they appreciated the opportunity to be involved in an 'enjoyable' activity with their child. All the mothers agreed that their children enjoyed the sessions and so did they. One of the mothers pinpointed the fun aspect of the involvement as being very important.

e)   One mother who admitted to being 'a busy working mum' said that often she felt a little guilty about doing chores and jobs around the house rather than spending time with her son. She felt that the weekly sessions provided a 'special' time which she could regularly put aside for her to be with her son and she told me that, in her particular situation, this was very valuable. Many of the mothers spoke about the importance of one-to-one close physical contact and the opportunity of being 'mother and child' in a situation other than at home. They said that it provided not only an emotional experience, but also a sense of security for their children.

f)   The mothers recognised the value of the therapy sessions not only for their children, but also for themselves. They met other adults in situations similar to themselves and made friends. This was very important to some of the mothers. One even involved her own friend in the therapy sessions and regularly brought her along to help out.

Conclusions to This Area of Study

When the mothers had spent about five minutes individually writing down what they felt were the benefits of their involvement in the Therapy Sessions, I began to encourage group discussion by asking the mothers what they had written. This stimulated comments from the other mothers and resulted in a conversation, the main points of which I have outlined in the previous section.

I was interested in finding out, not only the benefits the mums felt they derived from attending the sessions, but also the order of priority in which they would place them. All four mothers agreed that the most important benefit was an educational one. They valued the Music Therapy most highly and were delighted that their children were receiving it.

They saw their role as vital to this aspect of their children's education because they felt they provided a large proportion of the staffing needed for such a project. It is important to point out that the mother who did not attend the group discussion, but who popped in for just a few minutes, thought that 'doing something with him rather than leaving it to others and just coming to see what they do' was the most important factor.

6   Multisensory Approach—Action Checklist
1   Look at the needs of the group.
2   Read relevant books and articles and see relevant films.
3   Visit other schools and review their multisensory approach.
4   Educate and involve families and suitable volunteers.
5   Enlist the help of a music specialist.
6   Enlist the help of other professionals.
7   Plan the actual sessions to meet the group's requirements.
8   Keep the programme flexible and open to planned change.
9   Evaluate the sessions and work regularly.
10   Plan change and include everyone in both the planning and implementation.

7   Helpful Books, Articles, and Sources
Please refer to the main bibliography in Chapter 1 for general information that will help in developing a sensory curriculum and also help with recording and assessment of the curriculum.

HELPFUL INFORMATION SOURCES
For information on music therapy, contact:
The Secretary, Music Therapy Department, Harperbury Hospital, Radlett, Herts.

The Guildhall School of Music and Drama, Music Therapy Department, Barbican, London EC2.

BOOKS AND ARTICLES

Alwin, J. (1975). *Music Therapy.* John Clare Books.

Alwin, J. (1978). *Music Therapy for the Autistic Child.* Oxford University Press.

Argyle, M. (1967). *The Psychology of Interpersonal Behaviour.* Harmondsworth: Pelican Books.

Argyle, M. (1975). *Body Communications.* London: Methuen.

Argyle, M. (1979). *Person to Person—Ways of Communicating.* The Life Cycle Series. London: Harper and Row.

Berne, E. (1964). *Games People Play.* Harmondsworth: Penguin Books.

Fast, J. (1971). *Body Language.* London: Pan Books.

Grover, L. (1979). *Physical Education for Special Needs.* Contains chapter by Veronica Sherbourne. Cambridge University Press.

Leboyer, F. (1976). *Loving Hands.* London: Collins.

Levete, G. (1982). *No Handicap to Dance.* Human Horizons Series. London: Souvenir Press.

Morris, D. (1977). *Manwatching.* London: Jonathan Cape.

Robbins, N. (1975). *Music Therapy in Special Education.* London: Macdonald and Evans.

Upton, G. (1979). *Physical and Creative Activities for the Mentally Handicapped.* Contains three chapters by Veronica Sherbourne. Cambridge University Press.

Wood, M. (1982). *Music for Living.* Kidderminster: British Institute of Mental Handicap.

9 EXTENDING THE SENSORY CURRICULUM

Contents

1   Introduction

This chapter looks at the development, extension, and integration of the sensory curriculum into the whole school curriculum. It anticipates the very special child growing, becoming a very special student who requires a more adult environment and curriculum.

WHY EXTEND THE SENSORY CURRICULUM?

Some very special students will have begun to perceive the world around them with more depth and understanding. They may begin to realise that their actions may cause something interesting to happen in that world. For example:

— If I hit a balloon, it bobs up and down.
— If I make certain sounds, people react.
— If I smile, someone will smile back and encourage me.
— If I move my arm, the bells will jingle.
— If I roll over and stretch, I can reach the mobile.
— I can choose between milk and orange juice.
— I can smell food, so I turn towards the dinner table.
— I can pull the scarf off my face to see what is happening.
— I press a switch and interesting patterns and colours appear.

It must be stressed that, for many very special students, there is always a need for the sensory curriculum, as outlined in earlier chapters. Their complex and profound learning requirements mean that they are at a very simple level of development for a long while—perhaps for life. However, this should not preclude them from continuing their individual sensory curriculum within an appropriate environment, using curriculum materials suited to their age.

It would not be appropriate for the local sixth formers to learn in an infant school, using primary materials and curriculum. This is equally valid for the very special student. Such students should have equal access to all the facilities in their school, and beyond. The curriculum should be relevant to their needs, carefully planned, and properly evaluated. The students should not be merely passive observers.

The sensory curriculum continues to be used, but the settings change, the materials are different, and the approach more adult.

THE LINKS TO THE WHOLE SCHOOL CURRICULUM
The school curriculum should encompass all the educational requirements of every pupil at the school. This includes the very special student. The major areas of the curriculum may include:
—   Prerequisites to learning.
—   Movement.
—   Social and emotional development.
—   Total communication.
—   Cognitive/academic skills.
—   Living skills.
—   Creative curriculum.
—   Further education (for 16- to 19-year-olds).
Sensory curriculum can fit into all the above areas. If they are to dovetail with the whole school curriculum, then the following questions require clear answers:
    Is the school philosophy right for everyone?
    Will it cover basic skills at a realistic level?
    Must it adapt for those with added impairment?
    Has it sufficient scope?
    Are there clear targets and teaching plans?

Is it age appropriate?

Are the funds and resources available to implement the curriculum?

Extending the sensory curriculum into other specific educational areas can be developed in sensory science, prerequisites to learning, religious education and multisensory massage. Books on these topics are obtainable from:

Catalyst, 35 Send Road, Send, Woking, Surrey GU23 7ET.

DEVELOPING A WHOLE SCHOOL APPROACH

In developing a whole school curriculum, it is important to include all staff in its creation, including those involved with the very special students. This will ensure that the curriculum encompasses every pupil.

If the curriculum for special students is devised in isolation from the rest of the school, this will cause barriers. It will also then be difficult for the very special student to integrate into other areas and to use the whole school curriculum effectively.

Each curriculum should begin with the most elementary steps, so that the student's development is embodied in each area. This means that the special student's learning is held in esteem, has a common ground, has a shared understanding, and reflects mutual respect.

The curriculum should also be accessible for pupils with a specific learning requirement, for example, a blind child with a poor body image. As with any curriculum, some areas will be modified to suit a particular student, but the main framework should cover all aspects.

In order for this whole school curriculum to succeed, these are some of the points that may require consideration:

— the full backing of the Headteacher,
— endorsement of the Governing Body,
— involvement of the Local Education Authority adviser or inspector,
— parental involvement,
— a clear forward planning document,
— adapted physical resources,
— appropriate human resources,
— well maintained banks of resources,
— good resource bases,
— a common pupil profile,

— a common assessment,
— overlapping curriculum areas (the senses are in every area),
— group instruction as well as one-to-one teaching,
— age appropriate curriculum,
— regular review and evaluation of the whole curriculum,
— involvement of outside agencies, such as Area Health Authority, Social Services, and voluntary agencies,
— an alert interest in nationwide curriculum development.

AGE APPROPRIATE CURRICULUM

Despite his profound and complex learning difficulties, the very special student becomes older and more mature. As with any other person, there should be an increasing awareness of the need to accord respect and dignity at school, in the home, and in the community. This should be reflected in his surroundings at school.

The very special student should have the opportunity to progress through the school system as would any other pupil. The term 'special care' should have disappeared with other labels and be replaced with 'special educational requirements'. While he may require physical care during the day, the primary reason for attending school is *education*.

Awareness of the special student's more adult requirements should be reflected in the school curriculum. While he may be on a very simple sensory learning level, there are a variety of ways of teaching the senses in a more adult way. For example, the student may:

— learn taste and smell through a cookery lesson,
— understand bodily experience by riding a horse or sailing,
— find tactile stimulation on a nature walk,
— expand his range of sound by using a range of music tapes,
— Extend his visual stimulation in the computer room.

This more adult way of learning is also helpful for families or other care-givers, enabling them to realise that the very special child is growing up, with changing expectations and requirements. Look at the following range of age appropriate curriculum activities undertaken by very special students over a year. Reflected in all the activities are the senses. The very special students are active participants, not merely passive observers.

Wheelchair dancing
Pleasure park outing
Miniature railroad visit
Horse riding
Aeroplane ride to Legoland in Denmark for the day
Picking strawberries in the fields
Learning an Indian dance
Visiting the theatre for Atarahs Band
Taking part in a 'fun run' marathon
Taking part in a drama production for the whole school of
    'The Gingerbread Boy'
A visit to Sadlers Wells Ballet
A week on a working farm
A visit to a crisp factory
A visit to a health farm to use the jacuzzi
Steam train rides

Take just two of these activities and realise how the sensory curriculum is maintained in more adult surroundings as part of the age appropriate curriculum.

A Visit to the Ballet

Sound   A real orchestra, real instruments, crowd noises, clapping and cheers. Moving music, tapping of ballet shoes, rustle of the neighbouring seats, muted and hushed sounds prior to the performance start.

Vision   People nearby, looking down on the people below, looking up to the stage, bright arc lights, multicoloured light changes, stage fog, costumes, and twirling dancers.

Smell   The audience, stage smells, heat smells, the smell of people around you.

Taste   The ice-cream and drinks in the interval.

Bodily
Experience   The feeling of wanting to dance, moving to the music, getting up and down steps, using the elevator.

Multi-
sensory   The whole experience, i.e. including the trip in the minibus and the night journey home.

These sensations all combine to make an adult experience, using the senses to combine the whole effect into the central 'ballet' experience.

Riding a Horse

Sound   Enclosed sounds, barn noises, 'clip-clop' of horses' hooves, neighs, rustling of hay, voices with command, a horse chewing and drinking, patting the horse.

Vision   The helper's face, the bobbing up and down of horses, looking down on people, looking between the horse's ears.

Smell   'Horsey' smells, sawdust, hay, grass, horse food, apples, leather smells, horse's mouth and coat.

Taste   Grass, horse food, the horse's apple, and sometimes the horse!

Touch   A warm horse, a hairy tail and mane, a soft muzzle, patting and stroking the horse, feeling hay and sawdust, water, the helper's touch.

Bodily
Experience   Getting on and off the horse, controlling the horse, jogging, walking, bobbing up and down, jumping, abrupt stops, bumping and jumping around on the horse.

Multi-
sensory   the whole experience.

All these sensations combine to make a horse ride a blend of age appropriate sensory experiences.

INTEGRATING THE VERY SPECIAL STUDENT

It is now accepted 'good practice' to integrate pupils with

special educational requirements into a variety of educational settings, for a variety of curricula and for differing time spans. This integration is now beginning to extend to very special students, despite their complex and profound learning requirements.

The integration has to begin within the special school itself, with the breakdown of the barrier of the label 'special care provision'. Labels were removed from educational use by Warnock and the Education Act 1981, and this should have included the 'special care' label. While their physical needs require careful attention, very special children or students are primarily at school to receive an education in its fullest sense.

Integration can happen for these very special students and it can happen in a variety of ways which are similar to those experienced by more able pupils. It can be full-time, part-time, or intermittent. Integration can be justified for use of facilities or access to the main school curriculum and resources. It can also extend outside the special school into other educational settings, including the community at large.

As with any major innovation, integrating very special students must be carefully planned, evaluated and assessed on a regular basis. It is important to remember that the integration programme must take place gradually, over an agreed period of time.

The following list of points should be considered before embarking on any integration programme:

— Headteacher commitment.
— Staff commitment.
— Parental commitment.
— Board of Governors commitment.
— Local Education Authority commitment.
— Requirement for overall supervision by senior staff.
— Adequate staffing levels to enable smaller classes to accommodate a full-time very special student.
— Build-up of resources for access by the whole school.
— Establishment of home bases to house physical requirements, such as toilet facilities.
— Structural changes, if required.
— A home base in each major school area.
— A planning committee involving all areas of school life.

— Clear communication and discussion at every level with everyone kept in the picture.
— A common school curriculum.
— A common school evaluation of pupils.
— Use of specialist staff to back up the integration programme, e.g. speech therapist, music therapist, etc.
— A gradual change to integration, not a 'big bang'.
— Staff resource library in the very special child or student's area of education.
— Well planned, relevant courses for all staff on areas such as profound handicap, lifting, planning programmes.
— An overview of the national developments in integration.

Further sources of information can be found in:
Booth, T., and Potts, P. (1983). *Integrating Special Education.* Oxford: Basil Blackmell.
Hulley, T. *Samantha Goes to School, the Battle for Mainstream Integration.* Campaign for People with Mental Handicaps, 12A Maddox Street, London W1R 9PL.
Ouvry, C. (1987). *Educating Children with Profound Handicaps*, Section on Integration. Kidderminster: British Institute of Mental Handicap.

Information and help is also available from:
ACE (Advisory Centre for Education), 18 Victoria Park Square, London E2 9PB.
CSIE (Centre for Studies on Integration), SCOPE, 12 Par Crescent, London W1N 4EQ.

2 Computer Assisted Learning (CAL)
(*Acknowledgements to Myles Pilling*)
Microelectronics can enable very special students to extend their sensory curriculum through Computer Assisted Learning —CAL. CAL can extend their sensory learning in the following ways:
— developing learning beyond their physical body to reach their true potential,
— the use of high 'motivational' materials,
— improving two-way communication,
— increasing opportunities for independence,

— developing the understanding of cause and effect with
— simple problem solving,
— the use of self-directed leisure activities,
— developing choice and a right to choose,
— giving access to the rest of the school curriculum,
— developing preferences, likes and dislikes,
— giving a multisensory input—linking senses,
— presenting learning situations which can be repeated many times,
— setting individual goals at the student's own pace and level,
— the use of visual foreground/background, colour, special display size, and speed of movement,
— reinforcing current thinking,
— developing divergent thinking by open-ended programmes.

CAL can never replace the individual human-assisted learning experiences which very special students receive at school and elsewhere. There are some disadvantages which may be resolved in the near future with the increasing sophistication of current microelectronics. The disadvantages of CAL include:

— it requires additional electronic hardware,
— the computer peripherals are not interchangeable,
— the equipment is often bulky, and therefore not easy to transport,
— the equipment can be temperamental,
— the systems have a high cost of implementation,
— computer software (programs) is often crude and may require extensive modification, which is time-consuming and expensive,
— there are few suitable 'off the shelf' packages available,
— the computer model chosen often restricts the software that can be used.

These disadvantages do not prevent one from introducing a CAL programme, but do require that considerable planning and thought go into the initiation of such a programme.

Look at the flow chart in Fig. 9a which shows a school's computer curriculum. See how most areas can accommodate the very special student to enhance sensory learning. It is important to include the computer curriculum in the overall curriculum for the very special student.

Fig. 9a. Flow Diagram for Computer Curriculum
(Myles Pilling)

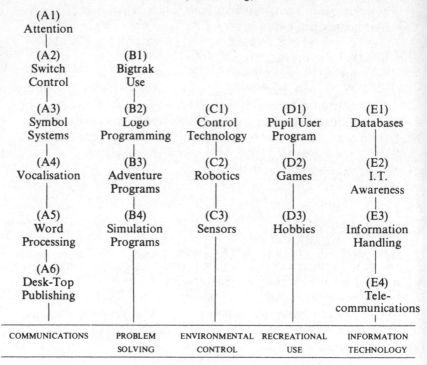

| COMMUNICATIONS | PROBLEM SOLVING | ENVIRONMENTAL CONTROL | RECREATIONAL USE | INFORMATION TECHNOLOGY |

The global aims of this computer curriculum also encompass the very special student. They may include:

Communication
   Microelectronics that can enable the profoundly handicapped to communicate to others and vice versa,
      or
   microelectronics that can enable those with fine-motor difficulties to write and communicate neatly, efficiently, and abundantly to others.

Problem-Solving
   Strategies that encourage logical thinking. The encouragement of sequential actions and events into a meaningful whole. The computer is an ideal means of achieving these aims.

Environmental Control
Control of environmental and household appliances via custom-made switches and computers for the profoundly handicapped.

Recreation
For the user to be able correctly and safely to operate microelectronic equipment.

To enjoy the independent use of playing games with others in school, with the student or his own friends, and in the family environment.

Computer Assisted Learning
The effective use of microelectronic devices across the whole curriculum for the following purposes:
— to reinforce current learning,
— to develop divergent thinking, i.e. open-ended programs that can express own thoughts, ideas, and needs, *and*
— to take the pupil from where he is to where he wants to go, i.e. individualised levels of learning and evaluation.

Information Technology
To increase the pupil's computer awareness to meet the future needs of our society in this technological age.

To be able to operate and interrogate simple information handling systems.

The environment needs careful control to enhance an extended sensory curriculum, especially in the visual and sound senses. Site, security, and safety are important factors. A suitable environment would be chosen for an individual and he would progress to other environments as he becomes capable of coping with more external distractions.

Below are listed eight environments for the use of Computer Assisted Learning. A very special student may require time to become familiar with any of them.
1 A complete blackout for full impact, e.g. a dark room.
2 A distraction-free room, the blind drawn and lights out.
3 A distraction-free room, natural light or lights on.
4 As above, with background music.
5 As above, with visual distractions.

6 An area in a classroom, screened off.
7 A classroom area, without screening.
8 The home environment.

Resources to reinforce the CAL programme can include:
— computer room,
— trolley of computer hardware,
— software library/catalogue,
— computer specialist on the staff,
— county computer staff,
— parent computer clubs,
— in-service training,
— computer stations around school,
— regional centres such as SEMERCS (special education microelectronic centres)
— computer 'partners' from other schools,
— development of materials through voluntary organisations,
— mainstream schools as centres for integration.

To show the importance of CAL to the very special student, look at the area of Communications for CAL in Fig. 9b. Fig. 9c expands on just one area of this model—vocalisation—showing how the computer can help in this sphere of learning. Fig. 9d shows the 'vocalisation' curriculum goal sheet in detail.

This area of communications is in early stages in the development of CAL. The application is there and, by the means of special microelectronic aids, quite sophisticated communication can occur. These aids include:

touch screen	voice activated	optical eye control
tongue switch	('micro mike')	concept keyboard
lever switch	photonic wand	sound operated switch
foot switch	suck and puff switch	light touch switch
chin switch	proximity switch	air-operated switch
tilt switch	pressure pad	

An excellent source of information on CAL aids and supplies is: *Communication Equipment for the Disabled* (1987), pp. 51-64.
Published by: Oxfordshire Health Authority, Mary Marlborough Lodge, Nuffield Orthopaedic Centre, Headington, Oxford OX3 1LD.

Software is available for use with CAL and can provide a sensory range of sound, moving pictures, and light stimulation from simple to complex, touch, vibration, and a combination of sensory inputs. Visual experience by means of complex, colourful and animated patterns can motivate the student to extend learning by looking, fixating, tracking, and close observation. Individual students' discs can be made from the software. Note: The software can be put in a 'loop' to repeat under their control, or as a holding technique. It can combine two sensations, e.g. a touch screen linked to activate a tape recorder with a recording of favourite sounds.

Fig. 9e shows a sample of a communication programme demonstrating the use of CAL to develop attention through eye contact.

Information on software, recording, and assessment is

Fig. 9b. Model for Computer Assisted Communication
(Myles Pilling)

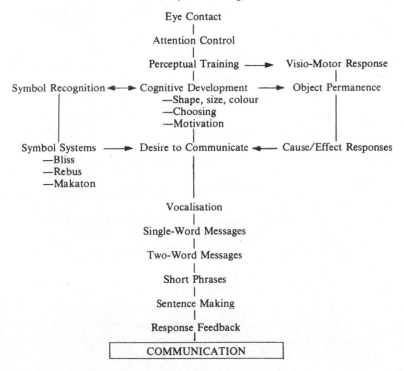

Fig 9c. Vocalisation Model in CAL Programme
(Myles Pilling)

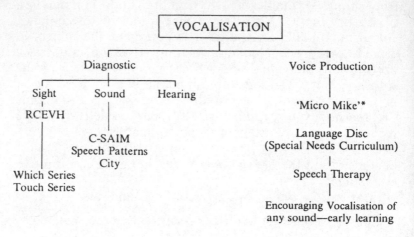

*'Micro Mike' obtainable from: Micro Mike, Silicon House, Fowke Street, Rothley, Leics, LE7 7PJ.

Fig 9d. Vocalisation Curriculum Objectives
(Myles Pilling)

Curriculum	:	Computer
Main aims	:	Communication
Goal	:	Vocalisation—to develop sound and voice production
Resources	:	Micro Mike

Objectives:
1 Will make a noise into the Micro Mike (not shy).
2 Understand cause and effect on a robot (turtle)—'nudge and trundle'.
3 Understand cause and effect on a screen—patterns and sounds.
4 Makes spontaneous noise to get a reaction.
5 Imitates consonants—sounds 'm' and 'b'.
6 Imitates sounds 'p', 't', and 'f'.
7 Sustains a sound 'aaaaaaah'.
8 Makes a sharp, sudden sound, e.g. 'Go!'.
9 Imitates vowel sounds—'a', 'e', 'i', 'o', 'u'.
10 Copies a rising and falling voice using City program.
11 Explores a variety of sounds spontaneously.
12 Imitates words on request.
13 Able to use a wide variety of vocalisations to control a game.

Fig 9e. Communication Curriculum Objectives—Attention
(Myles Pilling)

Curriculum : Computer
Main aims   : Communication
Goal   : Attention—to develop eye contact (stage 1)
Resources   : Dark room, comfortable seating very near the screen or robot, full screen brightness, dramatic program.

Objectives:
1   Indifferent to the screen or robot.
2   Fleeting physical reaction to the screen or robot.
3   Fleeting eye contact.
4   Fixates on the screen for a few seconds before eyes drift away.
5   Eye contact intently fixated on the screen for a few seconds.
6   Begins fleetingly to scan the screen or robot, for expected action *after* it is switched off.

Curriculum : Computer
Main aims   : Communication
Goal   : Attention—to develop eye contact (stage 2)
Resources   : Dark room, comfortable seating near screen or robot, full screen brightness, dramatic program.

Objectives:
1   Fixates eye contact on screen or robot for a few seconds.
2   Fixates and also begins to scan the screen or robot for a few seconds.
3   Scans and responds to dramatic movement, colour and sound.
4   Intently scans and responds for a measurable period of time.
5   Reacts when the screen or robot is switched off.

available from : Research Centre for the Education of the Visually Handicapped, University of Birmingham, Birmingham. And from: *Computer Assisted Development with Profoundly Retarded Multiply Handicapped Children.* Published by: Hillside House, Kilton Hospital School, Worksop, Nottinghamshire.

Assessment, through careful recording, is essential, as in all areas of the sensory curriculum. The Recording Sheet in Appendix C could be used, or a computer log book could be established, with the headings:

Date — Program — Child — Comments —
Response/Behaviour

Responses may be rated on a scale to simplify records. Physical reactions to the screen are the same as those which are observed in other sensory activities. The Kilton Hospital School manual gives a good range of responses that are coded to make simple recording possible. For example, the response to a child who is fixating on to a screen is coded from:

0   unable to keep awake for any period of time,

to

4   tracks display for a short time, up and down.

Useful publication:

A comprehensive range of free booklets concerning all aspects of hardware and software for special needs is obtainable from: NCET (National Council for Educational Technology), Sir William Lyons Park, Science Park, Coventry CV4 7EZ.

Hope, M. (1987). *Micros for Children with Special Needs.* Human Horizons Series. London: Souvenir Press.

10 INTEGRATING THE SENSORY CURRICULUM INTO THE WHOLE SCHOOL CURRICULUM

Contents

1 Introduction

In the last chapter the importance of an integrated and age appropriate curriculum was discussed. Such a curriculum should incorporate and extend the work in sensory curriculum undertaken by the very special student. Assessment, observation and evaluation are employed, in the same way as with the sensory curriculum the student is already undertaking. The aims and objectives remain similar; choice, however, should be prominent, e.g.
— choice of activity,
— choice of materials,

— choice to continue the activity, and

— choice to say 'no'.

Some sensory curriculum can be included in more conventional project work or thematic work for very special students. This approach can extend their sensory learning in the following ways:

— a 'whole' approach to learning, decreasing fragmented learning,

— the use of more than one sense to learn,

— active learning situations,

— widening horizons outside the classroom,

— heightening excitement,

— increasing motivation,

— work at different levels and paces, all contributing to a 'whole' project,

— use of all the processes of learning,

— diversifying and generalising everyday work,

— use of real contexts,

Fig. 10a. Example Project on the Sense of Touch

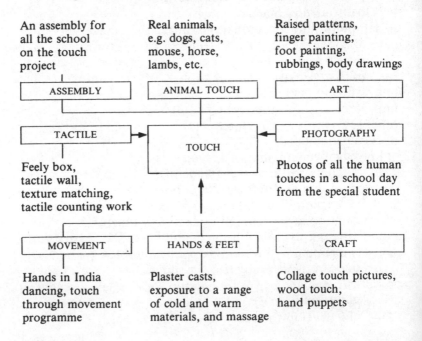

— the excitement of discovery,
— involvement of other students.

Look at the example project in Fig. 10a on the sense of touch, which could be undertaken by a group of very special students.

The following sections look at selected areas of the curriculum and explore the possibilities of incorporating sensory curriculum into these areas. The areas examined are:

— creative curriculum
— the living skills curriculum
— environmental science
— extending the touch curriculum

Always remember that the aims and objectives are the same as those described before, but the approach and materials are now different, age appropriate, and undertaken through the school curriculum.

The last section gives a brief outline of the use of Developmental Therapy to extend sensory learning and also to teach the ways of learning.

2   Creative Curriculum

It is important to ensure that this area of the curriculum is fully developed for the very special student. This is to ensure that an objectives-based approach does not dominate a school curriculum to the exclusion of creativity. It is meaningless and impossible to task-analyse the creative curriculum. It is just as important as any other area, enabling students to generalise other skills through its creativity. The senses dominate this part of the curriculum.

Look at the main aims of a creative curriculum listed below. They all apply to the special student:

— Fun and enjoyable motivation.
— Provision of a wide range of experiences for pupils to achieve a positive self image.
— The development of the potential of each student as an individual by providing opportunities to experience, to explore, and to express themselves.
— To provide a firm foundation for the development of personality.
— To develop the senses creatively.

— To reinforce, through the arts, all other areas of the curriculum.
— To promote creativity without necessarily an end product.

Fig. 10b illustrates how the creative and aesthetic arts can reinforce other areas of the curriculum.

The following are a range of practical suggestions and developments to incorporate extended sensory work in the areas of dance and music, just one creative area.

DANCE AS AN ART FORM
(*Courtesy of Christine Smith*)
If we are teaching dance as an art form, we are not merely teaching exercise to music. Therefore, lessons should not resemble aerobics, keep fit, disco, musical comedy, cabaret or

Fig. 10b. Expressive and Creative Arts

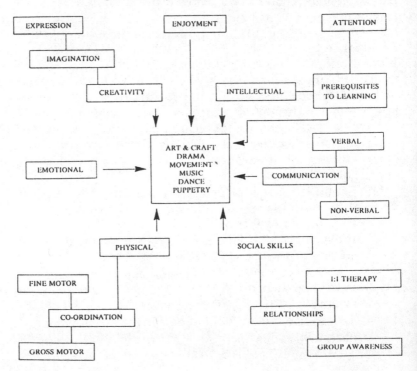

breakdancing classes. Elements of some of these forms of dancing may be used, but the aim is to teach dance as an art form.

The pupils need to know how to make, perform, and view dances. Therefore, we should promote:

— physical skills (or assistance) so that the pupil will be able to perform the dances adequately,
— knowledge of the material content or language of movement of dance,
— the ability to choose appropriate movement material and organise this into a coherent form to express or communicate an idea in dance terms,
— the ability to view dances critically and deepen the pupil's aesthetic appreciation.

The very special student may require a one-to-one or two-to-one assistance ratio for dance.

Why Dance

Dance can make a unique contribution to the education of every child. Dance gives an opportunity to acquire:

1 *Physical skills*
   a   It helps to make the child physically literate through improving co-ordination, increasing his movement vocabulary and by making him move in ways other than his habitual ones.
   b   A real enjoyment and an awareness of the body in action can be developed in the dance, thereby developing the child's bodily experience powers, i.e. realising how it *feels* to spin, leap, hover, etc.
2 *Creative skills* are developed through the composition of phrases and dances.
3 It develops a pupil's *thinking skills*, since composition requires, as a prerequisite, the ability to organise and plan.
4 It can develop the powers of *observation* through watching and working with others, thereby helping to increase an *aesthetic appreciation* of dance as an art form.
5 It gives an opportunity to *communicate* ideas through movement, rather than words.

6   It enhances *sensitivity* to:
  a   objects, e.g. other works of art,
  b   sounds, e.g. music, poetry,
  c   people—encourages co-operation through reading, following and moving in harmony with others, besides encouraging sensitivity to other people's ideas and feelings.
7   Dance can give a deeper appreciation of other curricular subjects by using these as a starting point or follow-up to dance activities.
8   Dance gives an opportunity for each pupil to work at his own level because he is not restricted by rules and regulations.

SOURCES FOR DANCE IDEAS

You must have a stimulus for your dance—something that arouses the mind or incites activity. As listed below, stimuli for dance can be auditory, visual, bodily experience, tactile or ideational.

Auditory Stimuli

Music
  Music can be used to indicate the overall form of the dance by suggesting its mood, style, phrasing, and length.
  Music can also be used as a springboard for another idea by using the quality or design or dramatic content which the music suggests.

Poetry or words
  Poetry can be used in the same way as music, i.e. you can dance with the poem or part of the poem as an accompaniment, or you can just use the idea behind the poem.

Percussion
  Percussion can be used rhythmically or for the quality of movement which different pieces encourage.

Human voice and body sounds

Sounds in nature or the environment
  For example, bird song, noise of water, sound of traffic, etc.

Visual Stimuli

From pictures, sculptures, patterns, shapes, etc., one can either take the idea behind the object,
or
use its lines, shapes, rhythm, texture, colour, or other imagined associations.

A chair, for example, could be used for its angularity, its purpose in holding the body weight, or it might be seen as a throne, a trap, an object to hide behind or under, etc.

Bodily Experience Stimuli

One can make a dance about movement itself. This might be a movement which you enjoy doing, e.g. turning or jumping, or a movement phrase, e.g. swoop, glide, hover.

One need not necessarily transmit any given idea, but it should have a dynamic range, pattern and form, for example, a dance inspired by animal movement.

Tactile Stimuli

Tactile stimuli can produce a bodily experience response which then becomes the motivation for dances, e.g. the smooth feel of a piece of velvet may suggest smoothness as a movement quality for a dance, or the feel and movement of a full skirt may promote swirling, flowing movements.

Tactile stimuli can also be generated by an accompanying object, e.g. a fine piece of material could be manipulated by the dancer as she moves, complementing, enveloping and following her.

Ideational Stimuli

Movement can be developed from an idea as in the following example, using the idea of 'the wind':

Type of wind	Movement idea (this can all happen in wheelchairs)
a gentle breeze	rising and falling, with drifting and floating sensation.
a gust of wind	sudden movement that travels to a new place.

a gale   continuous energetic movement with
                      jumps and leaps, using lots of space.
a whirlwind   strong turning, spinning and rushing.

Dance can also be made using the idea of wind effects on other
things, for example:
— people and other living creatures,
— plants, seeds, trees, and leaves,
— the sea and seashore,
— clouds,
— buildings, i.e. could demolish them or help windmills to
  turn their sails, etc.
— clothes on a washing line,
— balloons and kites.
All these effects will vary according to the 'mood' of the wind.

Ideas for Dance Using the Environment
(This would link to the environmental science curriculum.)
Weather
—thunder, lightning, rain, hail, snow, wind, frost, ice,
  sunshine, clouds, fog, etc.
Nature
—vegetation, i.e. plants and trees, forests, jungles, seed
  dispersal, etc.
—animal movement, including birds, fish, insects and reptiles.
—landscape, i.e. mountains, valleys, rocks, minerals, rivers,
  the sea, glaciers, caves, stalagmites, stalactites, sand
  dunes, deserts, waterfalls, coral reefs, etc.
—natural disasters, i.e. volcanoes, earthquakes, typhoons,
  forest fires, meteorites, floods, etc.
—found materials and objects, i.e. shells, twigs, pebbles,
  seed pods, horse chestnut cases, fossils, minerals, dandelion
  clocks, etc.
—planets, i.e. earth, sun, moon, stars, shooting stars,
  comets, etc.
The Seasons
—Winter: ice, snow, snowballing, making snowmen, footprints in the snow, Jack Frost, skating, and skiing.
—Spring: growth of plants and trees, birth and renewal,
  lambs, and sowing.

—Summer: sunshine, seaside, swimming, and movement of corn.

—Autumn: reaping and harvesting, withering and dying, and bonfires.

Creation
  —Earth
  —Air
  —Fire
  —Water
  —Animals

Helpful Books, Films and Addresses
Additional useful information in the area of dance is available from:

Astell-Burt, C. (1981). *Puppetry for Mentally Handicapped People.* Human Horizons Series. London: Souvenir Press.

Levete, G. (1982). *No Handicap to Dance* Human Horizons Series. London: Souvenir Press.

McLintock, A. B. (1984). *Drama for Mentally Handicapped Children.* Human Horizons Series. London: Souvenir Press.

Information on Sherbourne movement can be obtained from:
  Cyndi Hill,
  1 The Vale,
  Parkfield,
  Pucklechurch,
  Bristol BS17 3NW.

A list of colleges at which dance can be part of a course, dance schools, and a reading list is available from: Arts Council of Great Britain, Information Section, 105 Piccadilly, London W1V 0AV.

THE AREA OF MUSIC
(*Courtesy of Liz Clough, Music Therapist*)
The View of Music at St John's School
Music at St John's School is used in conjunction with all areas of the curriculum. It can encourage and develop skills throughout the whole range of learning, such as listening, responding to commands, working as a group, body awareness,

Fig. 10c. Expressive and Creative Arts—Music

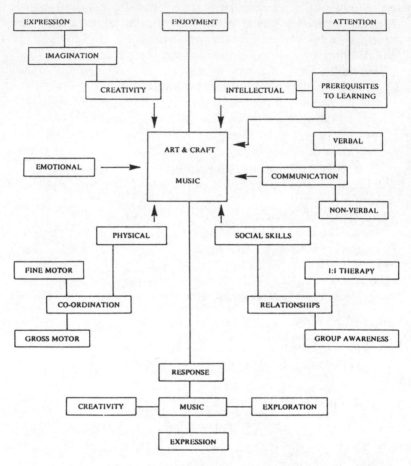

and confidence building. We work through the medium of sound.

The stimulus derived from creating sound is a primary objective. Secondary to this is the development of specific musical technique. For example, 'how' a drum is played is unimportant. The important factor is that a sound is being produced, and that it is an achievement and a means of expression. It is child centred, and a means of non-verbal communication. Every pupil in the school can contribute and achieve at their own level.

Music as a therapy is a specialised area, but many useful and enjoyable activities can be carried out by class teachers. Musical activities in the classroom should be used both to reinforce work covered by the music therapist, and to back up the development of skills throughout the curriculum.

The main aims of music include:
— to develop communication skills,
— to provide a means of non-verbal communication,
— to develop an awareness of the creation of sound,
— to develop a response to the basic elements and structure of music, i.e. pitch, dynamics, rhythm, melody, harmony, and timbre.

Fig. 10d. Musical Activities for Total Communication

Link to Curriculum Area	Suggested Activities	Age Appropriate Lower/Middle Upper School
Mouth control	Blowing instruments—melodica	
	harmonica	L
	whistles	M
	recorder	U
	Sing 'Everybody Do This'—open mouth	
	close mouth	L
	smile	M
	put out tongue	
	Sing 'babble' sounds to well known tune,	
	e.g. nursery rhyme tunes	L
	popular songs	M/U
	('la la la, ba ba ba, da, da, da', etc.)	
Response to sound or simple commands	Make sudden sound with interesting instrument such as hooter, whistle, drum, etc.	L/M/U
	Make quiet sounds, sustained sounds Track sound source up/down/left/right	L/M/U
	Game—Take turns locating 'hidden' sounds, behind screen or hidden anywhere in room	L/M/U
	Song—Rhythm of the music. Make up appropriate commands, e.g. 'Stand by the door' to the rhythm	L/M/U
	Song—Make up commands to fit any well known tune e.g. Mulberry Bush	L/M
Non-verbal communication	Eye contact—sing 'Hello' song	L/M
	—sing any popular song	L/M/U

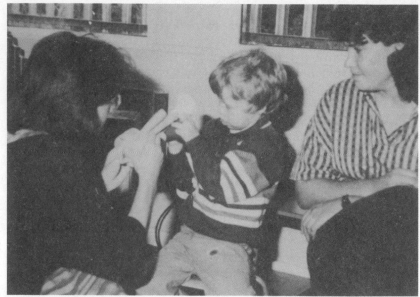

Tom explores the toy trumpet which has made a sudden loud noise (*above*), while Simon (*below*) responds positively to a loud noise from the trumpet which vibrates on his cheek.

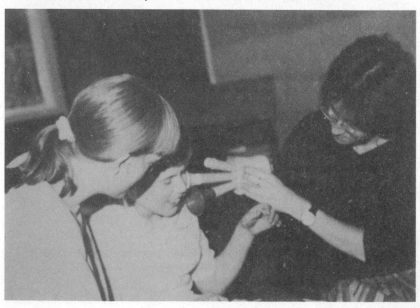

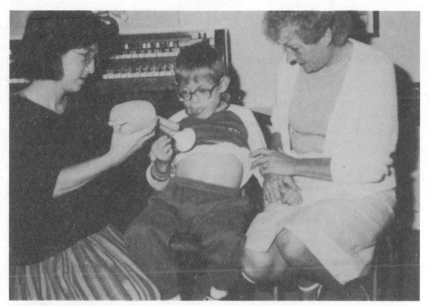

Paul anticipates a loud noise from the trumpet (*above*), and (*below*) concentrates on the vibratory feeling of the noise on his tummy.

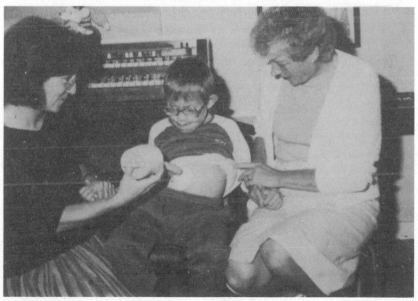

Fig. 10e. Musical Activities for Social and Emotional Behaviour

Link to Curriculum Area	Suggested Activities	Age Appropriate Lower/Middle Upper School
Body awareness	See Total Communication activities	
	Sing 'I can stretch up high'	L/M
	Sing 'Hokey Cokey'	U
	Exercise to a variety of music. Keep fit to music. See listening list for Pop	M/U
	Jazz	M/U
	Classical	M/U
	Relaxation to music.	L/M/U
Shows concern if injured or disturbed	NB. Certain sounds (generally high pitches) can cause pain to be registered. Please be aware of this if a pupil seems distressed/holding hands over ears, etc.	L/M/U
Enjoys centre of attention	Sing solo to everyone (add microphone, if possible)	L/M/U
	Play a special solo on a chosen instrument.	L/M/U
	Be 'conductor' of a group with instruments, i.e. pupil indicates to others when to play, stop, etc.	M/U
	Tape record these activities and play them back to the pupil.	L/M/U
Express opinion in group	Small group activity: each pupil chooses an instrument. Sit in a a circle. One pupil starts to play to another pupil. This must be indicated either by pointing, eye contact, or speech. Next pupil continues to play to someone else.	M/U
	Bongo drums 'conversation' between two pupils or pupil and adult. No speech is allowed.	L/M/U
	Choosing a favourite song.	

- to encourage spontaneity,
- to develop an awareness of self,
- to develop an awareness of each other in a group,
- to develop physical skills, social skills/emotional, communication skills, imaginative/creative abilities.

This can be more clearly seen in the flow diagram in Fig. 10c.
To illustrate how music can enhance the other curriculum

areas and extend sensory learning, Figs. 10d and 10e show two examples of musical activities. These incorporate the areas of communication and social and emotional behaviour into the music curriculum. They also enhance and extend the sense of sound and bodily experience.

Helpful Books and Music
Additional helpful sources of information for music curriculum ideas include:

Moog, H. (1976). *The Musical Experience of the Pre-School Child.* Schott and Co. Ltd.
Wood, M. (1983). *Music for Mentally Handicapped People.* Human Horizons Series. London: Souvenir Press.
Body and Voice (LD780). 70 music activities including three cassette tapes and a book with music and lyrics. Published by: LDA, Wisbech, Cambridge
Sing as You Grow (LD235 and LD271). 30 learning songs, cassette, and book. Published by: LDA, Wisbech, Cambridge
Language through Song (LD273). Simple songs about everyday activities. Book and tape. Published by: LDA, Wisbech, Cambridge

The tape and record library at your central library gives access to a very wide range of music and sound.

3   The Living Skills Curriculum
The school Living Skills Curriculum has the main aim of independence for life and may contain the following areas:
    personal hygiene
    personal appearance
    home care
    food skills
    health education
    first aid
    travel
    going out and about
    managing in the community
These are all important areas for the involvement of the very special student who will aim for his own level of independence, no matter what his specific individual limitations may be.

Here are practical suggestions for sensory integration into three areas of living skills—personal hygiene, home care and food skills. An outline of an individual personal presentation programme is also included, incorporating the area of health education.

PERSONAL HYGIENE

Parental permission should be sought before tackling many of the areas described here. Parents may also want to come in to school to work together with staff in this area. Living skills means more independence for the very special student. The student should have his own personal bag of materials and these should not be for communal use, for obvious health reasons.

Safety factors should be carefully observed. Work on a one-to-one basis is necessary in areas such as shaving or cleaning a bathroom.

Shaving

When using the implements and accessories for shaving, the student will have the following experiences and/or sensations:

feel of foam
taste of lather
tactile sensation of a razor
vibration of an electric razor
sensation of an electric razor on the skin
warm splashes of water
tracking the razor
bodily experience of helping with the shaving
sting of after shave lotion
smell of lather and after shave lotion

Now go to the local barber's shop to see others being shaved. Watch a male teacher shaving himself.

Washing hair

During the exercise of washing hair, the student will experience the following sensations:

smell of shampoos
choice of shampoos
feel of warm water spray

sensations on scalp, skin, and hair
smell of hair conditioners
feel and smell of bubbles and lather
bodily experience of helping wash hair
looking at hands, wet hair
feel of warm towel
massage of the scalp

Now go to the local hairdresser to see and experience a shampoo. Watch someone else wash her hair.

Drying hair
Following hair washing, drying the hair introduces the following new sensations:

tactile feel of towel
feel of damp hair
smell of damp hair
feel of hair dryer
choice of warm or cool heat setting
heat from the dryer on scalp and face
sensation of brushing and combing the hair

Go to the local hairdresser to see and experience hair drying done professionally.

Hair styling
During hair styling, the following sensations are experienced:

looking in a mirror and watching hair styling
choosing a hair style
hair spray smell during the styling
visual glitter of sprays
feel of hair styling gels.

Invite someone with a punk hair style to school to demonstrate a dramatic hair style to the students.

Using deodorants and perfumes
Selecting and using deodorants and perfumes involves mainly smells:

smells of a range of deodorants and perfumes
choice of a deodorant or perfume
tactile feel of roll-on, stick, or spray deodorant

bodily experience of helping with the deodorant or perfume

smell of sweat

Go to a chemist to select individual deodorants and perfumes. Allow for choice and individual preference for each student.

Bathing

Bathing is an essential life skill that involves a wide range of sensations. In the school, only parts of the body would be bathed, e.g. arms or legs. A complete bath would be done in the privacy of the home with parental assistance. Some of the sensations to be experienced are:

a range of soap smells

a choice of soaps

bubbles and bubble bath sensations

smells of additives to the bath

warm and cool water sensations

using a scratchy sponge or a smooth flannel

making the bubbles

bodily experience of helping wash

watching the omnipresent plastic duck bob on the water

Go to the local health centre and experience a sauna and/or jacuzzi.

Hand care

Caring for the hands involves interesting smells and tactile sensations, as well as bodily experience:

soap smells and choice of soap

feeling of lather and bubbles

massage of a range of hand creams

choice of hand cream and nail varnish

bodily experience of helping

rough vibration of emery board and nail file

smell of nail polish

watching nails being painted with glittery or fluorescent colours

hand massage with massage pad

Go to the manicurist or invite one to school to have hands done professionally. Go to the chemist to choose new materials— soaps, hand creams, etc.

Cleaning the teeth

Cleaning the teeth is another important life skill for good personal hygiene. It involves:

    choice of a range of toothpastes

    vibration of a battery toothbrush

    looking in the mirror after using disclosing tablets

    experiencing the different textures of various toothbrushes

    scratchy feel of tooth powder versus toothpaste

    following the toothbrush to the mouth

    bodily experience of helping clean the teeth

Arrange a visit to the dentist. Go to the chemist to choose toothpastes and toothbrushes.

HOME CARE

Very special students encounter some of the following experiences at home. They can participate and become involved with the various tasks at their own skill level.

Dusting and polishing

    smell of polish and dust in the air

    touch of the cloth, the dust

    bodily movement experiences in polishing, dusting, moving
      objects

    looking at the shine

    looking at the dirt

    following the movements of work

    remembering to put objects back in their proper places

Ask to be put on the rota for cleaning. Clean the Head's room to demonstrate how the student is learning home care skills. Go to the supermarket to choose various cleaning materials.

Cleaning the bathroom

    feel of warmth and steam

    bathroom smells of soap, shampoo

    the bodily experience of scrubbing and polishing

    feel of scratchy cleaning pads

    listening to the water, the cistern, gurgling

    reaching down into the bath

    reaching up to the mirror

    looking at the mirror and spraying it with cleaner

experiencing soapy suds
the touch of rubber gloves on the hands
bodily experience of mopping, wiping, scrubbing
Now go to the bathroom in someone's house and clean it. This
is probably a one-to-one teaching exercise as most bathrooms
are small. Go to the supermarket to select the correct cleaning
materials.

Vacuuming a room
listening to the noises of the vacuum cleaner
sucking up different objects
feeling vibration
feeling hot, dusty air
smelling the dusty air
bodily movement of pushing and pulling the cleaner
Try the caretaker's large vacuum cleaner. Work with one of the
cleaners who regularly does the vacuuming.

Washing clothes
varying noise of the washing machine
smell of clean linen versus dirty linen
sorting and putting clothes into piles
tactile feel of clothes wet and dry, different textures
bodily experience of lifting, pulling out, pushing
vibration of the washing machine
go outside to hang up clothes
watching clothes go round and round in the machine
Go to the local launderette. Offer to wash the tea towels from
the staff room on a regular basis—they will begin to appreciate
the living skills curriculum.

Washing dishes
smell of bubbles and soap
looking at swirling water
hot steamy atmosphere
taste of bubbles
feel as the bubbles pop
noise of banging crockery, tinkling cutlery
touch of the warm water and cold rinse
choice of helping to wash or dry

Offer your group to wash staff coffee cups once a week in the staff room. Find a dishwasher and experience a different way to clean the dishes. Go to the school kitchen and watch the staff wash up on a regular basis.

FOOD SKILLS
This area may include the following objectives:

flavours	smells	basic skills
drinking	hot/cold drinks	sandwiches and toast
can opening	diet	shopping
lay and clear table	preparing vegetables	eating out
manners	one-step cookery	two-step cookery

The food skills curriculum can take place in the classroom, moving out to the home economics area, the school flat, and finally an ordinary kitchen. It can also generalise into the community by visits to cafés, the local pub, or to a self-service restaurant. The curriculum should also include trips to the local shop or market to buy ingredients.

Here are some practical suggestions for sensory integration into two areas—flavours and one-step cooking.

Flavours
The presentation of a wide range of flavours is now taken out of the classroom and learnt in new situations. These may be:

    a vending machine
    an ice cream van
    a chainstore self-service restaurant
    the railway buffet
    a bistro
    the local café
    the local pub
    a visit to someone else's home

These locations also ensure a choice of flavours, allowing the very special student to make his own food-related decisions.

Fig. 10f shows the flavours section for an objectives sheet for food skills. A list would be kept of all the situations in which the skills have been involved throughout the year. This list would build up over the years, generalising the sensory taste and smell curriculum into many situations.

Fig. 10f. Food Skills Objectives List

Curriculum	: Living skills
Main aim	: Food skills
Goal	: To accept different flavours and textures
Resources	:

Objectives:	Identified Foods
1 Is able to show preference for certain foods.	
2 Is able to show preference for certain drinks.	
3 Is able to refuse food if dislikes.	
4 Is able to refuse food if full.	
5 Is able to take a hot drink.	
6 Is able to take a warm drink.	
7 Is able to take a cold drink.	
8 Is able to take cold food.	
9 Is able to take hot food.	
10 Is able to take warm food.	
11 Is able to take sour food.	
12 Is able to take sweet food.	
13 Is able to take savoury food.	
14 Is able to take a fizzy drink.	
15 Is able to eat fruit.	
16 Is able to eat chocolate.	
17 Is able to eat crisps.	
18 Is able to eat sweets.	
19 Is able to eat ice-cream.	
20 Other.	

Places Visited:

One-Step Cookery
One-step cookery can be undertaken in the classroom, extended to the home economics area, and then carried into a home kitchen. It is not necessary to actually cook with heat to have a successful cooking programme. A Belling portable cooker is an asset if you do want to cook in the classroom. Here is a range of sensory cooking experiences possible without heat, mainly on a one-to-one basis, with human assisted learning.

exploring cooking tools with water (cups, bowls, hand beaters),
tasting fresh fruit,
scrubbing with brushes (carrots, celery, potatoes),
tearing, breaking, snapping (lettuce, pea pods),
pouring (oils, milk, water),
pouring dry ingredients (rice, corn meal, dried peas),
stirring (cake mix, carrots into salad cream, etc.),
spreading with a finger or knife (butter, honey, syrup),
shaking (cream for butter, colouring coconut),
rolling with both hands (cheese balls, sausage meat),
juicing with a hand juicer (oranges, lemons),
peeling with fingers (oranges, eggs),
cracking open (raw eggs, nuts),
cutting with a table knife (from soft food to hard food),
grinding with hand grinder (coffee, peanuts),
beating with egg beater (eggnog, meringue),
peeling with a scraper (carrots, potatoes),
grating with a hand grater (cheese, carrot),
listening to snap, crackle, pop (popcorn),
looking at popcorn popping out of the pan,
rubbing (fat into flour),
sifting (flour, icing sugar),
touching—everything,
smelling—everything,
tasting—everything.

This wide range of activities gives a new dimension to taste and smell.

One-step cooking involves recipes which have one main ingredient or require only one step to prepare. This is to ensure simple sequencing and a nice, quick, eatable result to reinforce the experience. The special student can make his own lunch. Positioning is important, to enable the student to see and do as much as possible. A 'buddy' system often helps.

Recipes can include:

popcorn	popcorn and oil (pan and heat)
milk shake	milk and shake mix (mixer)
toast	bread and butter (toaster)
tinned soup	soup tin (pan and heat)
instant whip	whip mix and milk (mixer)
orange squash	orange squash mix and water (container)
lemon tea	instant tea mix and water (pan and heat)
peanut butter	prepared peanuts (hand grinder)
pasta	pasta and water (pan and heat)
cocoa	cocoa and milk (pan and heat for hot cocoa)
eggnog	eggs and milk (container and hand whisk,
orange juice	real oranges (hand juicer)
lemonade	lemons, water and sugar (juicer and container)
instant cake	cake mix and water (pan and mixer)
peppermint creams	icing sugar, water, and mint essence (container)

Families are thrilled when cookery goes home, even if it is an instant cake. There is always great anticipation from the students, as cookery means a nice food gratification at the end of the exercise.

PERSONAL PRESENTATION ACTIVITIES
(*Courtesy of Barry Kemp*)
The following section contains curriculum ideas for personal presentation activities.

Personal Presentation Activities Scheme

Pupils	:	Seven very special students, age range 13-17.
Staff	:	One teacher and one assistant, plus the school nurse.

Aims
1 Practising self-help skills in an appropriate setting.
2 Experiencing age appropriate health education activities in adolescence.
3 Experiencing personal presentation activities.
4 Experiencing sensory curriculum activities in an appropriate setting.

Content
1 Self-help skills.
   a) Teeth cleaning.
   b) Hand washing.
   c) Face washing.
   d) Hair brushing.
2 Age-appropriate health education activities.

Boys		*Girls*	
a)	Shaving	a)	Hand cream
b)	Using deodorant	b)	Nail varnish
c)	After shave	c)	Perfume
d)	Hair style	d)	Hair style
		e)	Jewellery

3 Personal presentation activities.
4 Activities are defined as 'personal presentation activities' when carried out with the adult in order to improve the social acceptance of the pupil with regard to appearance.
4 Sensory curriculum activities.
   The activities can be viewed as having sensory components, as shown in the Table overleaf.

Method
Session : Tuesdays 1.45-3.00 pm.
Venue : Washrooms and lobby, Senior Department.
Staff : Teacher, assistant, school nurse, visiting student teacher, volunteer.
Pupils : Donald (to 2.15 pm)—goes to Living Skills group.
Clare (to 2.30 pm)—goes to CAL group.
Edward (to 2.50 pm)—goes to Music Therapy.
Kersty, Karen, Kevin, Susan—make up core group.

Procedure
1   The pupils' abilities at undertaking activities can be placed on the following continuum:

Personal presentation activities   Self-help skills

◄───►

Maximal help   Minimal help

(Kersty, Karen) (Donald)   (Clare) (Edward) (Susan)

2   The individual pupil should be given the opportunity to progress from personal presentation activities to limited or complete self-help skills.
3   The content of the self-help skills shall be the task analysis contained in the Living Skills Curriculum and subsequent teaching based on performance levels.
4   Individual pupils shall be assessed using the relevant assessment sheets and weekly sessions should be based on those assessments contained in the main school curriculum.

4   Environmental Science
The main aim of environmental science, incorporating the very special student, is to provide situations which increase

TABLE—SENSORY COMPONENTS OF PERSONAL PRESENTATION
ACTIVITIES

Sensory Stimulation

Activity	Visual	Smell	Taste	Tactile	Sound	Bodily Movement
Hand washing	✕	✕		✕	✕	✕
Teeth cleaning	✕	✕	✕	✕	✕	✕
Face washing	✕	✕		✕	✕	✕
Hair brushing	✕			✕	✕	✕
Shaving	✕			✕	✕	✕
Hand cream	✕	✕		✕		✕
Nail varnish	✕	✕				✕
Aftershave	✕	✕		✕	✕	✕
Perfume	✕	✕			✕	✕

awareness and responses to the environment and allow the student to exercise influence over it.

This is a most exciting area of the curriculum for very special students. It covers areas that are interesting to explore and provides a range of planned activities which they may not have encountered before. This part of the curriculum begins to help them make sense of the world around them by encouraging the beginning of logical thinking.

Curriculum areas in environmental science may include:

gardening	the sea
animals	the seaside
country environments	night and day
insects	trees
water	shiny objects
seasons	noise
plants and flowers	minibeasts
weather	mud
baby animals	things that fly
birds	the sun
ourselves	autumn leaves
the senses	snow
fish and ponds	

Well planned resources are important to back up work in this area. It is nice to know that the sensory banks can be used by the rest of the school to supplement their own introduction to environmental science. Other pupils will learn from the materials the very special student uses every day.

One way to utilise the sensory bank materials is to have investigation tables set up for use by all students. Here are examples of three investigation tables.

Air Investigation Table
This resource could include:

air pump	tyre	football bladder
model aeroplanes	ball inflator	kites
parachute	propeller	windmill
feathers	sink plunger	hand fans
electric fan	streamers	hair dryer
bicycle inner tube	rubber sucker toys	'whoopee' cushion
empty spray bottle	drinking straws	blowers

Sound Investigation Table
This resource might contain the following items:

bells	whistles	musical milk bottles
musical toys	metal spoons	wooden blocks
stethoscope	tin and string telephone	metal tubes
humming top	tapes of sounds	squeakers
alarm clock	range of paper noises	range of drums
bird warblers	siren	electric organ
bubbler pipe	container with beads	tape recorder

Light Investigation Table
The light table could contain:

magnifying glass	lenses (concave/convex)	binoculars
telescope	wide range of mirrors	diffraction box
mirror box	distorting mirror	shiny spoons
sheets of acetate	range of glass prisms	spinning colour discs
torches	fibre-optic torch	strobe lights
Christmas lights	box of glittering materials	

The school loaned their sensory materials to a primary school who were undertaking a primary project themselves. The special students then visited and joined in, too.

Below are listed some areas with practical suggestions and activities enhancing sensory learning. Sensible precautions should be taken with animals, especially mouth-sized morsels like snails! A helpful booklet is also available from: Centre for Life Studies, Zoological Gardens, Regent's Park, London NW1 4RY.

Slugs and Snails
Collect slugs and snails on a rainy day:
touch them,
watch them move,
track them with a torch,
watch them eat,
see them leave a silvery trail,
watch them climbing a window,
tickle them,
make a snail tank,
photograph them,
make up a slug noise song.

Worms
Dig up some worms:
  feel them wriggle,
  watch them slither,
  track them with a torch,
  tickle them and see how they move,
  fill old stockings with sand to make a 'worm',
  make puppet worms,
  photograph worms,
  make up a worm song.

Caterpillars
Collect a variety of species:
  touch them,
  watch them curl up,
  let them crawl on your hand,
  keep some in a tank,
  make egg box caterpillars,
  make a caterpillar puppet,
  photograph them,
  (play dough makes lovely caterpillars).

Trees
Adopt a tree in the school grounds or in a nearby park and use
it in the following activities:
  Build up a photo collection of the tree through the year with
    the pupils in the picture.
  Picnic and tell stories under 'your' tree.
  Collect the seeds and grow them.
  Look at the leaf litter and find insects, fungi, skeleton leaves.
  Take rubbings from the trunk of the tree.
  Look under the bark and see what you can find.
  Make your own tree in the class.
  Look at the leaves—press them, make plaster casts and clay
    casts.
  Make boot polish prints.
  Conserve the seeds and throw them into treeless areas from
    wheelchairs.
  Bring in the autumn leaves to make leaf mobiles and collage
    pictures.

Gardening

A group of very special students did the following over a school year:

Grew herbs outside and dried them, hanging them from the classroom ceiling.

Grew alpine strawberries in pots so that they could be placed at different levels and the students could pick and eat them as they were able.

Grew small salad vegetables, in a redundant sand tray and stand, at just the right height for wheelchairs.

Made a portable garden of pot-grown plants such as geraniums, fuchsias, petunias and Busy Lizzies, so that they could be brought inside for the winter.

Cuttings were taken from the plants.

A range of scented geraniums was grown for the smell table and dried bowls of herbs placed there, as well.

Herbs were used to make herb scones.

Visits were made to garden centres to buy what was required.

Visits were made to flower shows and people's gardens.

You could also grow your own wild flower meadow in a protected area of the school grounds.

Animals

Have an animal on loan, for all to care for.

Bring animals into school. (One class had visits from a chicken, dog, kittens, rabbit, a rat, budgie, gerbil, lamb, piglet, donkey and goat).

Stay on a farm for a few days.

Have a rabbit project, studying habits, food, feel, habitat; make a collage of rabbits, nurture the rabbit, etc.

Farmcraft, a family holiday and education centre, welcome very special students and make special provision for them. Contact them at Farmcraft, Shipley Country Park, Heanor, Derbyshire DE7 7JS.

Hind Leap Warren Activities Centre, Wych Cross, Forest Row, Sussex RH18 5JS. They run Earth Education activities to allow very special people to develop an empathy with the natural environment through the senses, feeling, and understanding. Earth walks and concept

pathways generate a sense of awe and wonder of even the
most simple things in nature.

The P.A.T. Dog Scheme will arrange regular visits for an
owner and well-trained dog to pay visits to your school.
Contact them at Rocky Bank, 4 New Road, Ditton, Kent
ME20 6AD.

Get the *Animals of Course!* series by Jill Bailey, published by
William Heinemann Ltd. which includes 'Mouths', 'Noses',
'Eyes'.

Mud

Remember, very special students like to make a mess, too!

Make a mud pile outside the school and play in it.

Fill the water tray with mud and make mud pies.

Make mud footprints and handprints.

Squish, squash and squeeze it!

Smell it. (Some may even try to taste it!)

If there is no mud available, fill a tray or bowl with potting
soil or tree bark or sand plus water.

Drop things into mud to see the effect and hear the sounds.

Make your own mud with sawdust, wallpaper paste and
water. Salt preserves it, so make models.

Make 'mud pie cake' using chocolate cake mix.

Country Parks

Country wardens will take you on nature trails if booked in
advance.

Roll in the leaves in the autumn.

Go pond 'dipping' for feeling and smelling the contents of a
pond.

Go on bat walks with a batometer.

Feel (and sometimes taste?) different barks of trees, leaves,
berries and fruits.

Make collages of the things you find on the walks.

Push wheelchairs through the woods (this may be bumpy,
but cushions help).

Fly kites from the top of a hill.

Look at a rotten log and all the types of insects it contains.

Turn over stones, feel and watch the 'creepie crawlies' which
squirm or run away.

Additional Helpful Resources
Here are some more helpful books and other resources for the environmental science curriculum:

Jones, A. V. (1983). *Science for Handicapped Children.* Horizons Series. London: Souvenir Press.
Northamptonshire County Council (1982). *Five Senses Project.* An introduction to the five senses, including the sense of taste, smell, hearing, sight and touch. Published by Northamptonshire County Council.
Pluckrose, H., and Fairclough, C. (1985). *Think about Series*, including 'Touching', 'Tasting', 'Smelling', 'Seeing and Hearing'. London: Franklin Watts.
Purnell, R. (1987). 'What Sort of Science', in *Special Children*, March 1987, pp. 16–17.
Tunnicliffe, S. D. (1987). 'Special Materials for Special Needs', in *British Journal of Special Education*, June 1987, pp. 73–5.
Tunnicliffe, S. D. (1987). 'Steps into Science', in *Child Education*, April 1987, pp. 42–4.
Read and Do Series, including 'Touch and Feel', 'Ears and Hearing', 'Taste and Smell', 'Eyes and Looking' (lovely photographs). London: Arnold-Wheaton.

Additional sources of information are available from:
Centre for Life Studies, Zoological Gardens, Regent's Park, London NW1 4RY.
Topics: snails, ourselves, earthworms, the senses, fresh water, the food chain, animal coverings, small mammals, incubating and hatching eggs.

The Association for Science Education publish *Primary Science* every few months, containing many ideas which could be modified for use with very special students. Details are available from: The Association for Science Education, Bookselling Department, College Lane, Hatfield, Herts. HL10 9AA.

Also contact Friends of the Earth, the Boy Scouts, Brownies, and local environmental groups such as the Wildlife Conservation Society. They will all be eager to help in this curriculum area. The local Rotary Club will give a list of friendly Rotarians who will welcome visitors, e.g. pet shop owners, land owners, building supervisors, farmers, etc.

For another useful monthly news sheet, contact Council for Environmental Education (CEE), School of Education, University of Reading, London Road, Reading RG1 5AQ.

5   Extending the Touch Curriculum

The very special student requires a tactile programme which takes into account the maturity of the student. Just as it is not appropriate for a teenager to hug and kiss a stranger, it is inappropriate for a very special student to be handled and touched like a baby. A teenager should shake your hand in greeting, and a very special student should likewise receive a tactile programme as a dignified adult.

Touch —identifies,
      —conveys unspoken words,
      —stimulates,
      —relaxes,
      —warns of danger,
      —demonstrates affection,
      —relaxes the body,
      —relaxes the mind,
      —polarises energy, and
      —bonds people together.

This can be incorporated in an age appropriate curriculum in the areas of massage, aromatherapy and communication through contact.

MASSAGE

Massage is the art of touching. It can be of benefit, especially to the physically handicapped student with continually tensed muscles or body parts. Massage can stimulate the blood flow to the tensed areas of the body, deliver nutrients to the muscles and help them to relax and loosen. One class of very special students have a hand or foot massage at the beginning of the school day to relax them after a long bus ride to school.

The most common form of massage is by use of the hands. A variety of materials can be used to massage the skin, and there

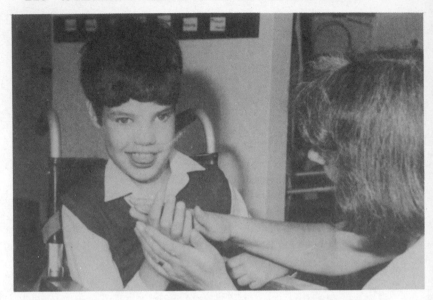

Ian enjoys hand massage (*above*), using peppermint lotion. He can both smell and feel the experience. (Below) he concentrates on his hand and the massage.

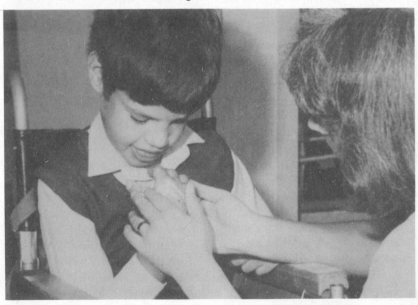

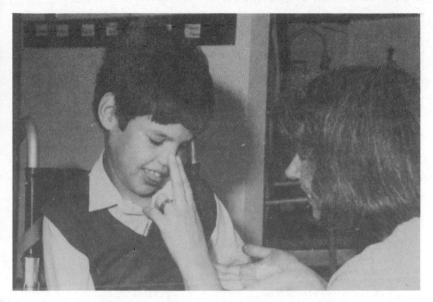

(*Above*) he experiences an unexpected massage on his nose,
and (*below*) gets his own back!

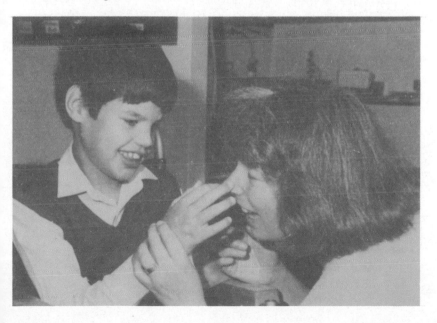

is the added bonus of the feel and smell of the massage materials. There are aids to massage which include the electrical facial massager, manicure massager, and vibrating foot massager.

Here are some practical suggestions for massage materials. Many can be obtained from the chain of shops run by Body Shop International, Dominion Way, Rustington, West Sussex BN16 3LR. These shops also provide an excellent opportunity for a sensory visit, especially in the area of smell, for the very special student.

Face Massage
   Useful materials for facial massage include:
      neck gel,
      Japanese washing grains,
      Viennese chalk facial wash,
      lip balms,
      carrot facial oils,
      range of facial toners, and
      astringents.
   Give the student a choice of materials.
   Invite a beautician in to school to demonstrate facial massage.
   Go to a health farm for a range of massages.

Body Parts Massage
   Useful materials include:
   rich massage lotions,
   body massage lotion,
   Johnson's baby oil/lotion,
   range of handcreams,
   peppermint foot lotion,
   sensitive skin lotions,
   herbal body shampoo,
   coconut butter oil,
   hair gels.

Massage Aids
   Body buddies—rubber massage mittens.
   Skin towels—friction rubs.
   Skin sponges—soft texture.

Loofahs—rough texture.
Pumice stone—hard.
Boots the Chemists do a range of sports towels, friction rubs.

An example of massage is the
Polarity Therapy Massage
This simple massage is nice and relaxing, used after swimming
or physiotherapy.

1   Rub hands together for about a minute until quite hot.
Massage oil can be used.
2   Press hands gently on student in this order:
—on the base of the neck and spine,
—on the sides of the head,
—on the forehead and stomach,
—on one hip and shoulder,
—on other hip and shoulder,
—on right foot and left hand,
—on left foot and right hand.
3   Keep rubbing your hands to create warmth and empathy.
4   At the end of the session, shake hands vigorously to
discharge static.

Information on extending massage into a curriculum can be found
in: Longhorn, F. (1993). *Planning a Multisensory Massage
Programme for Very Special People*. From Catalyst, 35 Send
Road, Send, Woking, Surrey GU23 7ET.

AROMATHERAPY
Aromatherapy links touch with smell. The use of aromatic oils
to enhance health and good feeling through massage dates
back to 4,500 BC. The oils are all natural and contain the scents
of flowers, leaves, herbs, roots and bark. They have different
effects: peppermint has a cooling effect on the skin; tangerine is
an energiser; rose is soothing and antiseptic.

It is advisable to contact the local aromatherapist in the area,
who can advise on the combinations of oils suitable for each
very special student. They are usually located at health farms
or beauty salons.

Further information can be obtained from The International Federation of Aromatherapists, Department of Continuing Education, The Royal Masonic Hospital, Powers Court Park, London. W6 OTN.

Essential oils are obtainable from: Jade College of Natural Therapy, 12 Jenkyn Road, Wootton, Bedfordshire MK43 9HE.

G. Baldwins and Co., Medical Herbalists, 171/173 Walworth Road, London SE17 1RW.

Additional sources of information include:

Tisserand, R. (1985). *The Art of Aromatherapy*. C. W. Daniel Co. Ltd.

Tisserand, M. (1985). *Aromatherapy for Women*. Thorsons Publishers.

Sanderson, H., Harrison J. and Price, S. (1991). *Aromatherapy and Massage for People with Learning Disabilities*. Hands On Publishing.

Courses and products from:

Shirley Price Aromatherapy, Upper Bond Street, Hinckley, Leics. LE10 1RS.	Stock a wide range of essential oils and other products.
Jade College of Natural Therapy, 12 Jenkyn Road, Wootton, Bedfordshire MK43 9HE.	Run courses on massage and aromatherapy and supply essential oils.
Hands On Publishing and Training, 9 Poplar Road, Kings Heath, Birmingham B14 7AA.	Courses especially for special needs in massage and aromatherapy.

EXTENDING TOUCH THROUGH CONTACT PROGRAMMES

Very special students will be participating in body awareness programmes to heighten their awareness of themselves. The multisensory programmes using music, touch and movement can be extended in a variety of adult ways.

These can include:

Relationship work through *Sherbourne sessions* which involve teaming up with a more able student. The areas of trust, caring and group work are encompassed, as well as many new bodily experiences.

Yoga can be undertaken with a volunteer yoga teacher from the community. This includes relaxation and breathing exercises. Some very special students may require two helpers for their yoga movements. It must be stressed that the yoga programme would be carefully planned and assessed by the yoga teacher in conjunction with the physiotherapist and class teacher. A helpful book is *You and Me Yoga System* by M. Gunstone, published by You and Me Yoga Centre, The Cottage, Burton in Kendal, Carnforth LA6 1ND. It includes a video and colour system to teach yoga to special people.

Keep fit and aerobic sessions are an enjoyable means of encouraging the relationship through touch and movement linked to sound. The programme has to match the very special student's ability and be carefully monitored by the aerobic teacher and physiotherapist. The music in these sessions is full of modern, bouncy tunes and is a great motivator. Tapes are obtainable from any record or department store.

The work of *Marianne and Christopher Knill* provides activity programmes which can be used for sensory, perceptual and movement skills, all linked to communications. They can be modified to suit particular requirements. There are three parts to the materials:

1   cassette tapes with music and instruction to accompany the activities, which are invaluable if there is no access to a music specialist.
2   a very detailed and pictorial handbook of the six programmes.
3   assessment and recording forms for the evaluation of reactions to help plan future approaches.

Again, the music element is important, acting as a motivator, enabling closer contact and forming a base for fun and play in the relationship work.

Details of the programme are available from LDA, Wisbech, Cambridgeshire.

Knill, M., and C. (1986). *Activity Programmes for Body Awareness, Contact and Communication.* Published by Living and Learning (Cambridge) Ltd.

6 Developmental Therapy

Developmental Therapy originates from the United States, set up by Professor Mary Wood at the University of Georgia. It is in use at three or four schools in the United Kingdom. A greatly modified therapy has been developed at St John's School, Bedford, to extend the learning of very special students. An integral part is sensory learning.

WHAT IS DEVELOPMENTAL THERAPY?

Developmental Therapy is a psycho-educational curriculum, organised around the sequence of normal developmental milestones. The therapy is a GROWTH MODEL rather than a deficit model. It looks at what a student can do in order to succeed and learn, and builds on this. It concentrates on the area of social and emotional growth.

There are four basic curriculum areas:
Behaviour
Communication
Socialisation
Cognitive

Within each of these areas is a series of measurable developmental objectives which are sequenced into five stages of therapy. The very special student fits into the objectives at all stages.

Stage 1   To respond with pleasure.
Stage 2   To respond with success.
Stage 3   Learning skills for successful participation.
Stage 4   Investing in group processes.
Stage 5   Generalising individual and group skills.

Development therapy incorporates and extends sensory learning at the same time as it teaches the very special student how to learn. The most important asset of the programme is that it is tremendous fun; no one fails—and that includes the leader of the session.

It is also exciting for very special students to begin to learn about group participation. Much of their education has to be on a one-to-one basis and the importance of being a valued member of a group experience is neglected.

The main points of Development Therapy in relation to the very special student are:

— it uses the senses to learn,
— it looks at what a student can *do* in order to feel success, pleasure and confidence,
— it follows the normal pattern of development to expedite the therapeutic process,
— it does not isolate a student from the mainstream of normal experiences,
— it has an in-built evaluation system,
— it is not dependent on a student's verbal or cognitive ability,
— it can be used on a one-to-one basis or in a group situation.
— the technique is so different and has the ability to get a response from the student for him to succeed,
— students succeed at every step,
— the system of co-active, reactive and preference learning is used at any stage,
— physical contact communicates to the student that you care about what he is doing,
— it is broad enough to cover any serious emotional or behavioural problem exhibited by the student,
— consistency in programme experiences, i.e. predictable, simple, familiar repetition of experiences, is essential, conveying security,
— every aspect is planned,
— it is a product of staff effort,
— it has clear, defined expectations.

The following is an outline of a typical Developmental Therapy session with very special students participating:

Group : six very special students.
Staff : one teacher, one assistant, one student volunteer.
Length : 50 minutes (this time has gradually built up from 20 minutes).

Main Aims:
 —to look
 —to listen
 —to be aware of others
 —to complete a given task
 —to follow simple instructions.

Activities:

Hello time	A 'hello' to each individual is sung.
Drawing time	Sing actions for up and down, round and round, with paper taped to the table to prevent accidents.
Work time	Select an activity in the sensory area for each student to complete.
Exercise time	Each student uses a large therapy ball, helped by staff.
Snack time	Choose from the food and drink offered.
Clearing table	Clear and wipe the table.
Music	Imitate rhythms or vibrations and use of instruments.
Carpet time	Move to another area of the room for story and people-sized puppets.
Floating cloud	Back to the table to be enveloped in a gauze cloud with an anticipatory song.
Toilet time	
Goodbye time	A group goodbye to each individual, then outside to play.

There is a musical link between each activity, telling clearly what the student should expect. This gives the experience of anticipation and security. Music quickly serves to bring back into the group any student who is not attending. They respond to music, as everyone has some sort of rhythm in their body—even just by moving about. Time is allowed for students with the most complex learning difficulties to respond, even if fleetingly.

There is a detailed assessment profile to monitor progress, concerning the four major areas. Further information can be obtained from Christine Smith, St John's School, Austin Canons, Kempston, Bedford, Beds.

Here are some useful books for further information:

Bacharach, A. W., Mosley, A., Swindle, F., and Wood, M. M. (1978). *Developmental Therapy for Young Children with Autistic Characteristics.* Baltimore, Maryland: University Park Press.

Purvus, J., and Samett, S. (eds.) (1976). *Music in Developmental Therapy.* Baltimore, Maryland: University Park Press.

Williams, G. H., and Wood, M. M. (1977). *Developmental Art Therapy.* Baltimore, Maryland: University Park Press.

Wood, M. M. (1975). *Developmental Therapy.* Baltimore, Maryland: University Park Press.

APPENDIX A
SAMPLE SENSORY QUESTIONNAIRE

SCHOOL

Child: _____   Date: ___/___/___

During the next couple of weeks we shall be working with your child, especially with his/her sense of *sound*.

You know your child best of all. Therefore, we would like your help in planning a Sound Programme for your child for the coming term. Assisting us will be the teacher for the hearing impaired and the music specialist, as well as the speech therapist. We would especially like to know what *you* would like your child to achieve in this area of development.

If it is possible for you to come in to school for a few minutes during the next couple of weeks, we would like you to join in with a sound lesson with your child. In this way, we can all learn together.

Sound sessions take place on _____ .

We do hope that you can come and participate. Thank you for your continued help.

SOUND QUESTIONNAIRE (FROM HOME)

Child: _____   Date: ___/___/___

Person(s) completing the questionnaire: _____
   Will you help your child do some 'homework' in this area if
   we send some home? (YES/NO)
   If the answer is YES, please try, by questions and/or
   observations, to help provide the following information
   about your child and *sounds*.

Sounds I like:

Sounds I do not like:

My happy sounds:

My sad sounds:

Sounds I make myself at home:

Special home sounds to which I respond
(eg. Dad singing in the bath, a pet, etc.):

Music, jingles, songs, rhymes,
or instruments to which I enjoy listening:

Music, jingles, songs, rhymes,
or instruments which I do not like:

Sounds you would like to learn or enjoy:

Any further comments:

Home Teacher: _____
Date received: ___/___/___

APPENDIX B
SAMPLE 'HOMEWORK' CARD FOR THE
SENSORY AREA OF SOUND

SCHOOL HOMEWORK CARD

Child's Name: <u>Bob</u>   Date: <u>1 Nov 1984</u>

Homework Area: Sounds

Reason for Homework: Bob has been learning about the different sounds of water at school.

How it will help: Bob may begin to listen for sounds of water at home as well and may begin to realise each water sound has a meaning.

Homework   1 Put Bob near the washing machine when it is on, tell him what is making the sound—water.

2 Take a jug into the bath with Bob and let him feel and hear the water sounds.

3 Let Bob hear the water being poured to make a cup of tea—tell him what the sound is.

Record—Please write here *anything* that has happened over the week, even if nothing has!

Return this card to school when you are finished. Well Done! and Thank You!

Homebase Teacher: _____

Date received: ___/___/___

APPENDIX C
SIMPLE RECORDING AND ASSESSMENT

This Appendix contains three examples of simple recording sheets.

The following list of books and articles may also be helpful in choosing a suitable method of observation or assessment of the very special child. There are also references to sources for recording and assessing in each individual chapter. Before using any of the materials, it would be wise to seek the help of other professionals, such as the school psychologist, in choosing methods that will be of maximum use for the whole school group.

Anderson, C. A. (1983). *Feeding—A Guide to Assessment and Intervention with Handicapped Children*. Obtainable from: Publications Department, Jordanhill College of Education, Southbrae Drive, Glasgow G13 1PP.

Anson House Project (1979). *Checklists Used at Anson House Pre-School Project*. Anson House Pre-School Project Research Paper. Obtainable from: Hester Adrian Research Centre, University of Manchester.

Bailey, I. (1983). *Structuring a Curriculum for Profoundly Mentally Handicapped Children*. Obtainable from: Publications Department, Jordanhill College of Education, Southbrae Drive, Glasgow G13 1PP.

British Institute of Mental Handicap (1983). *The Paths to Mobility Checklist*. Obtainable from: British Institute of Mental Handicap, Wolverhampton Road, Kidderminster, Worcs. DY10 3PP.

Brazelton, T. B. *National Behavioural Assessment Scale*, Clinics in Dev. Medicine, No. 88. Oxford: Blackwell Scientific Publications.

Browning, M. M. *et al.* (1983). *Identifying the Needs of Profoundly Mentally Handicapped Children.* Obtainable from: Publications Department, Jordanhill College of Education, Southbrae Drive, Glasgow G13 1PP.

Curtis, W. S. (1985). *Observational Evaluation of Severely Multiply Handicapped Children.* Manchester: Haigh and Hochland.

Clift, P. (1981). *Record Keeping in Primary Schools.* Schools Council Research Studies. London: Macmillan Educational.

Jones, M., Reid, B., and Kiernan, C. (1983). *The Environmental Assessment Schedule and Manual.* Published by the Thomas Coram Research Unit, University of London, Institute of Education.

Kershman, S. M., and Napier, D. (1982). 'Systematic Procedures for Eliciting and Recording Responses to Sound Stimuli in Deaf Blind Multiply Handicapped Children', in *Volta Review*, May 1982, pp. 226–37.

Kiernan, C. (1981). *Assessment of Programmes for Teaching.* Globe Educational.

Kiernan, C. (1987). *Pre-Verbal Communication Schedule.* Windsor: NFER/Nelson.

Kiernan, C., and Jones, M. (1977). *Behaviour Assessment Battery.* Windsor: NFER/Nelson.

Knill, M. and C. (1986). *Activity Programmes for Body Awareness, Contact and Communication.* Chapter 4— procedures for assessment and recording progress in body awareness, contact and communication. Published by LDA.

Morgenstern, F. (1981). *Teaching Plans for Handicapped Children.* London: Methuen.

Sebba, J. (1980). *A System for Assessment and Intervention for Pre-School Profoundly Multiply Handicapped Children.* Obtainable from: Barnardo's, Tanners Lane, Ilford, Essex.

Stevens, M. (1978). *Observe—Then Teach: An Observational Approach to Teaching Mentally Handicapped Children.* London: Edward Arnold.

Simon, G. B. (1981). *The Next Step on the Ladder: Assessment and Management of the Multi-Handicapped Child.* Published by: British Institute of Mental Handicap, Wolverhampton Road, Kidderminster, Worcs. DY10 3PP.

Warner, J. (1981). *Feeding Checklist*. Obtainable from: PTM, 23 Horn Street, Winslow, Bucks. MK18 3AP.

Webb, R., Shultz, B., McMahill, J. *Glenwood Awareness, Manipulation and Posture Index*. Published by: Glenwood State School, Glenwood, Iowa, USA.

SCHOOL

Child's Name: _____   Week of: ___/___/___
Curriculum Planner: _____

	achieved	repeat	finished
1.			
2.			
3.			
4.			
5.			

Comments:

SCHOOL

Sensory Area: _____ Name: _____

	Materials	Date	Exposure	Response	Comments
1.					
2.					
3.					

DAILY TIME LOG AND ANALYSIS SHEET

Page	Day	Date	Month	Year

Start Time	Finish Time	Activity	ACTIVITY	CATEGORY						

Summary   Hours

                 Minutes

                 Day total

SCHOOL

Curriculum Area : _____

Main Aim   : _____

Goal   : _____

date commenced	method reward	date mastered	date checked	OBJECTIVES
				1.
				2.
				3.
				4.
				5.
				6.
				7.
				8.
				9.
				10.
				11.
				12.
				13.
				14.
				15.